Family Food in 2004-05

A National Statistics Publication by Defra

LONDON : TSO

Published with the permission of the Department for Environment, Food and Rural Affairs on behalf of the controller of Her Majesty's Stationery Office.

© Crown copyright 2006

All rights reserved.

Copyright in the typographical arrangement and design is vested in the Crown.
Applications for reproduction should be made in writing to the Copyright Unit, The Stationery Office, St Clements House, 2-16 Colegate, Norwich NR3 1BQ.

First published 2006

ISBN 10 0-11-243092-9
ISBN 13 978-11-243092-6

A National Statistics Publication

National Statistics are produced to high professional standards set out in the National Statistics Code of Practice. They undergo regular quality assurance reviews to ensure that they meet customer needs. They are produced free from any political interference.

For general enquiries about National Statistics, contact the National Statistics Customer Contact Centre on **0845 601 3034**
minicom: 01633 812399
E-mail: info@statistics.gov.uk
Fax: 01633 652747
Post: Room D115, Government Buildings
           Cardiff Road, Newport NP10 8XG

Published by TSO (The Stationery Office) and available from:

Online: **www.tsoshop.co.uk**

Mail, Telephone, Fax & E-mail

TSO, PO Box 29, Norwich, NR3 1GN
Telephone orders/General enquiries 0870 600 5522
Fax orders 0870 600 5533
Email customer.services@tso.co.uk
Textphone 0870 240 3701

TSO Shops

123 Kingsway, London WC2B 6PQ
020 7042 6393 Fax 020 7242 6394
68-69 Bull Street, Birmingham B4 6AD
0121 236 9696 Fax 0121 236 9699
9-21 Princess Street, Manchester M60 8AS
0161 834 7201 Fax 0161 833 0634
16 Arthur Street, Belfast BT1 4GD
028 9023 8451 Fax 028 9023 5401
18-19 High Street, Cardiff CF10 1PT
029 2039 5548 029 2038 4347
71 Lothian Road, Edinburgh EH3 9AZ
0870 606 5566 Fax 0870 606 5588

TSO Accredited Agents
(see Yellow Pages)

and through good booksellers

Executive Summary

1 Family Food 2004-05 is the latest in a series of annual reports published by Defra on food and drink purchases in the United Kingdom based on the Expenditure and Food Survey. The report presents latest trends in purchases by type of food. Trends in energy and nutrient content of the purchases are also presented, based on a database of nutrient profiles for different types of food which are kept up to date by the Food Standards Agency.

Expenditure

2 Average expenditure on all food and drink in the UK in 2004-05 was £34.31 per person per week. Of this an average of £6.20 per person per week was on alcoholic drinks and an average of £28.11 per person per week on food and non-alcoholic drinks. Overall expenditure on food and drink was estimated to have been 2.1 per cent higher in 2004-05 than in the previous year, a 1.0 per cent drop in real terms. Expenditure on food and drink eaten out was 3.0 per cent higher in 2004-05 which in real terms was broadly unchanged.

3 There was a 3 per cent increase in purchases of higher value added products such as pre-prepared salads and organic produce in 2004-05.

Energy intake

4 Average energy intake per person in the year to March 2005 was 1.8 per cent lower than a year previously, continuing the long term gradual decline in energy intake.

5 Eating out accounted for 8.5 per cent of energy intake in the year to March 2005. Alcoholic drinks contributed 13 per cent of energy from eating out. After excluding alcoholic drinks, eating out contributed 7.6 per cent of energy intake. Energy intake from food and drink eaten out was estimated to have been 6.8 per cent lower in 2004-05 than a year previously and 10 per cent lower than in 2001-02.

Comparison with dietary recommendations

6 The percentages of food energy intake derived from fat, saturated fatty acids and non-milk extrinsic sugars were all above the recommendations made in 1991 by the Committee on Medical Aspects of Food and Nutrition Policy (COMA) of the Department of Health.

7 The percentages of food energy derived from fat and saturated fatty acids show no statistically significant change since 2001-02. There was no trend in the percentage of food energy derived from non-milk extrinsic sugars since 2001-02.

8 Quantities of fruit and vegetables purchased for the household show no statistically significant change since 2001-02.

9 There was a downward trend since 2000 in intake of sodium based on household purchases, excluding sodium from table salt. However intake of sodium in 2004-05, even when excluding sodium from table salt and excluding sodium from food purchased for consumption outside the home, was above the maximum intake for adults of 6g salt per day (2.4g sodium per day) recommended by the Scientific Advisory Committee on Nutrition. Analysis of urine collections provides a more robust estimate of sodium intake and sodium intakes are being monitored by separate surveys using these methods.

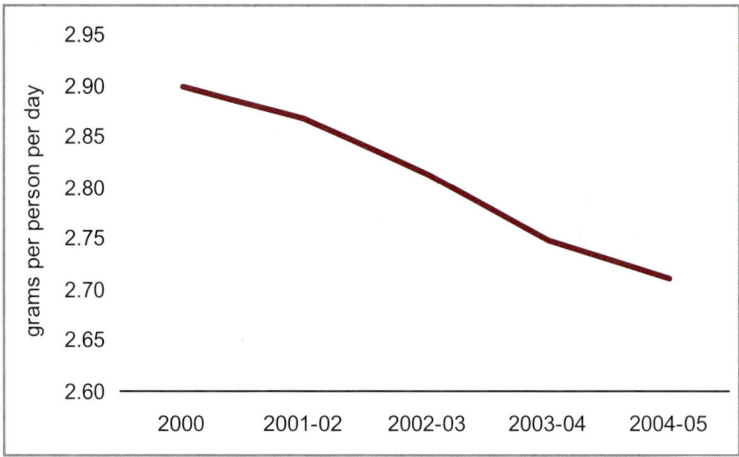

Downward trend in sodium intake since 2000

10. Requirements for nutrients have been estimated and called dietary reference values. The reference nutrient intake (RNI) is the dietary reference value sufficient for nearly all members of a group. If the average intake for a nutrient is below the RNI, the implication is that the nutritional needs of at least some healthy persons in the UK population are not being met.

11. The 2004-05 survey shows that magnesium and potassium intakes were below the weighted RNI at 94 per cent and 87 per cent respectively. Intakes of all other minerals and vitamins were above the weighted RNIs.

Significant dietary changes

12. There were reductions in purchases of whole-milk, cooked bacon and ham, fresh and processed potatoes, frozen vegetables, white bread, soft drinks and alcoholic drinks. There were rises in purchases of skimmed milks, fromage frais, other fresh vegetables and wholemeal bread.

13. Whole-milk consumption has been in decline since 1974. Quantities of purchases of confectionery for consumption outside the home have fallen in each of the three years since 2001-02. The quantity of alcoholic drinks purchased for consumption outside the home has fallen steadily each year since 2001-02 and was 16 per cent lower in 2004-05 than in 2001-02. However between 1994 and 2004-05 household purchases of alcoholic drinks rose by 38 per cent. The quantity of fresh and processed potatoes purchased for the household and for eating out fell in each of the three years since 2001-02.

Regional and demographic patterns

14. The Expenditure and Food Survey has an annual sample of about 7000 households which is large enough to enable regional and some demographic analysis. To improve the robustness of the comparisons the three most recent years of survey data (2002-03, 2003-04 and 2004-05) are averaged together.

15. Quantities of fruit and vegetables (excluding fresh and processed potatoes) purchased for the

household were highest in England and lowest in Northern Ireland. Quantities of fresh and processed potatoes purchased for the household were highest in Northern Ireland and lowest in Scotland. Scottish households purchased the most soft drinks. Expenditure on alcoholic drinks (i.e. including both household and eating out purchases) was highest in England and lowest in Northern Ireland.

16 Household purchases of vegetables (excluding fresh and processed potatoes) were lowest in the North West of England and highest in the South West of England. The North East had the lowest household purchases of fruit and the East had the highest. Expenditure on alcoholic drinks (i.e. including both household and eating out purchases) was highest in Yorkshire and the Humber and lowest in the East. When eating out, households in London purchased the most Indian, Chinese and Thai meals, and Yorkshire and the Humber purchased the most fish products and fresh and processed potatoes. Eating out expenditure as a percentage of overall food and drink spending was 38 per cent in London and 30 per cent in the East compared with 33 per cent across England as whole.

17 Household members in the lowest income quintile had the lowest intakes of alcohol but also the lowest intakes of vitamin C. Adult only households spent 7.2 per cent more than the UK average on food and drink eaten at home and 25 per cent more on eating out. Members of households where the Household Reference Person was aged under thirty spent 43 per cent of their food and drink budget on eating out while the "75 and over" group spent only 19 per cent of their food and drink budget on eating out. Intakes of most vitamins and minerals were lowest in households where the Household Reference Person ceased full time education at the age of 16. The percentage of food energy derived from saturated fatty acids decreased as the age at which the Household Reference Person left full-time education increased. Household purchases of vegetables were lower in households where the Household Reference Person was classified as "Never worked and long-term unemployed" than in the households where the Household Reference Person was in employment.

Contents

Executive summary	v
Preface	xi
Chapter 1 Family Food in 2004-05	1
Chapter 2 Key Trends Informing Policy	13
Chapter 3 Trends in Household Purchases	21
Chapter 4 Trends in Household Expenditure	33
Chapter 5 Trends in Household Nutrient Intakes	43
Chapter 6 Food and Drink Purchased for Consumption Outside the Home	49
Chapter 7 Geographic Comparisons	57
Chapter 8 Demographic Comparisons	71
The Family Food Committee	107
Development Issues	108
Links to the Family Food Website	111

Preface

1. In producing Family Food 2004-05 Defra have been assisted by the Family Food Committee, the Food Standards Agency, the Office for National Statistics and The Department of Health.

2. The figures presented in Family Food 2004-05 are sourced from the Expenditure and Food Survey, a survey that is also the data source for the Office for National Statistics' Family Spending report. The survey started in April 2001, and was preceded by the National Food Survey and the Family Expenditure Survey. In 2004-05 the Expenditure and Food Survey collected the diaries of 16,257 people within 6,798 households across the United Kingdom. Each household member over the age of seven years kept a diary of all their expenditure over a 2 week period. Note that the diaries record expenditure and quantities of purchases of food and drink rather than consumption of food and drink. Mis-reporting is a problem with all dietary surveys but is considered to be lower in the Expenditure and Food Survey due on the one hand to its focus on expenditure and on the other hand that everyone over seven years old completes a diary.

3. The Expenditure and Food Survey is effectively a continuation of the Family Expenditure Survey extended to record quantities of purchases. Estimates from the National Food Survey from 1974 to 2000 have been adjusted by aligning estimates for the year 2000 with corresponding estimates from the Family Expenditure Survey. Whilst estimates of household consumption from the National Food Survey have been adjusted a break in the series in 2001-02 remains and should be borne in mind when interpreting reported changes between the years up to 2000 and the years 2001-02 and beyond.

4. The estimates of quantities purchased are converted into energy and nutrient intakes and provide the best estimates available of trends in intakes, some going back to 1940. The trends are based on nutrient profiles of the edible components of different types of food and drink but make no allowance for wastage of edible components. When average intakes are compared with reference nutrient intakes a very approximate figure of 10 per cent is used for wastage of all types of food and drink.

5. Reliable estimates of food and drink eaten out start in 2001-02 when the National Food Survey was replaced by the Expenditure and Food Survey. Less reliable estimates of food and drink eaten out are available from the National Food Survey back to 1994.

6. Confectionery, alcoholic drinks and soft drinks brought home are included in household food from 1992 onwards. In 1996 the survey was extended to include Northern Ireland. Free food such as school meals and work-provided meals and snacks is not included in the estimates since 2001-02. Occurrences of free food are recorded in the survey and estimates will be made for future reports.

Further information

7. An electronic version of the report and accompanying datasets, many with fuller details than in this report, can be found free of charge on the family food page of the statistics section of the Defra website at: http://statistics.defra.gov.uk/esg/publications/efs/default.asp

8 The Defra team producing this report and managing the quality of the food statistics would welcome feedback to familyfood@defra.gsi.gov.uk

9 Defra co-fund the Expenditure and Food Survey with the Office for National Statistics who published their report on the survey, "Family Spending 2004-05", on 29 November 2005 at: http://www.statistics.gov.uk/downloads/theme_social/Family_Spending_2004-05/FS04-05.pdf

Chapter 1 Family Food in 2004-05

Headlines

- average energy intake from all food and drink was 1.8 per cent lower in 2004-05, continuing the long term gradual decline

- eating out purchases fell in 2004-05, which translated into a 6.8 per cent reduction in energy intake from eating out

- eating out accounted for 8.5 per cent of energy intake in the year to March 2005; reducing to 7.6 percent of energy intake if energy from alcohol was excluded

- average expenditure on all food and drink in the UK in 2004-05 was £34.31 per person per week

- average expenditure on food and drink brought home was £23.05 per person per week in 2004-05, 1.4 per cent lower in real terms than the previous year

- expenditure on eating out (including alcoholic drinks) was £11.26 per person per week in 2004-05, which was 3.0 per cent higher than the previous year

- there was a 3 per cent increase in the overall value added of food and drink purchases in 2004-05, e.g. more pre-packed vegetables

- quantities fruit and vegetables (excluding potatoes) purchased were hardly changed in 2004-05 at only 0.2 per cent higher

- there is a downward trend in intake of sodium since 2000, based on household purchases of food and drink excluding purchases of table salt

- the quantity of alcoholic drinks purchased for consumption outside the home was 7.3 per cent lower than the previous year and 16 per cent lower than in 2001-02

- quantities of wholemilk and fresh and processed potatoes purchased for the household showed reductions, continuing longer term trends

- household purchases of fruit and vegetables (excluding fresh and processed potatoes) were highest in England and lowest in Northern Ireland

- household members in the lowest income quintile had the lowest intakes of alcohol but also the lowest intakes of vitamin C

This chapter looks at the results of the 2004-05 Expenditure and Food Survey and compares estimated intakes, purchases and expenditure on food and drink in the United Kingdom with the previous year. Longer term trends are presented in later chapters.

Energy intake in 2004-05

1. Table 1.1 shows estimates of energy and nutrient intakes in the UK in 2004-05 derived from food and drink purchases including alcoholic drinks.

2. Average energy intake per person in 2004-05 was 1.8 per cent lower than a year previously, continuing the long term gradual decline in energy intake (see also chart 2.2). Energy intake from food and drink eaten out was estimated to have been 6.8 per cent lower in 2004-05 than the previous year and 10 per cent lower than in 2001-02.

3. Eating out was estimated to have contributed 8.5 per cent of overall energy intake in 2004-05. Alcoholic drinks were a significant source of this energy, contributing 13 per cent of energy from eating out. After excluding alcoholic drinks, eating out contributed 7.6 per cent of energy intake.

Nutrient intakes in 2004-05

4. With a decline in average energy intake per person there is an associated decline in average nutrient intakes. However, changes in intakes are generally small from year to year and are not statistically significant.

5. Only three of the nutrients recorded showed a rise in average intake in 2004-05 whilst over twenty showed a fall. The largest falls were in vitamin A, vitamin B12, vitamin C, vitamin E and alcohol. Longer term trends are presented in Chapter 5.

Percentage energy from macronutrients

6. The percentages of food energy (i.e. excluding alcohol) contributed by macronutrients (e.g. fat, carbohydrates, proteins), from both household supplies and eating out, are valuable measures allowing comparisons between groups with different levels of energy expenditure and/or intake. In 1991 the Committee on Medical Aspects of Food and Nutrition Policy (COMA) recommended that population average intakes of different macronutrients should not exceed specified limits. For example the population average intakes of total fat, saturated fatty acids and non-milk extrinsic sugars (principally added sugars) should not exceed 35 per cent, 11 per cent and 11 per cent of food energy respectively. In 2004-05, as in previous years, the percentages of food energy contributed by the various macronutrients were above the recommended limits.

Intakes from eating out in 2004-05

7. In general nutrient intakes from eating out were lower in 2004-05 than a year previously, in line with the fall of 6.8 per cent in intake of energy from eating out.

8. For most nutrients the contribution to average daily intake from eating out was between 6 and 10 per cent. Alcohol is the exception with roughly one third of people's intake coming from alcoholic drinks purchased for consumption outside the home, the remainder coming from household supplies.

Table 1.1 Estimated UK average energy and nutient intakes from food and drink in 2004-05 (a)

		Household food	Food eaten out	All food and drink	% change in all food and drink since 2003-04	% from food eaten out
					intake per person per day	
Energy	kcal	2 048	191	2 239	- 1.8	8.5
	MJ	8.6	0.8	9.4	- 1.8	8.5
Energy excluding alcohol	kcal	1 998	165	2 163	- 1.8	7.6
Vegetable protein	g	27.5				
Animal protein	g	43.1				
Total Protein	g	70.6	5.8	76.5	0.8	7.6
Fat	g	83.4	7.2	90.6	- 2.1	8.0
Fatty acids:						
Saturates	g	32.9	2.5	35.5	- 2.4	7.1
Mono-unsaturates	g	30.2	2.8	33.0	- 1.9	8.5
Poly-unsaturates	g	14.6	1.4	16.0	- 1.9	8.7
Cholesterol	mg	230	23	253	- 3.0	9.1
Carbohydrate (b)	g	257	21	278	- 1.8	7.4
Total sugars	g	123	11	133	- 2.1	8.0
Non-milk extrinsic sugars	g	80	9	89	- 2.7	10.3
Starch	g	134	10	144	- 1.6	6.8
Fibre (c)	g	13.2	0.9	14.1	+ 0.3	6.3
Alcohol	g	7.2	3.6	10.8	- 4.3	33.5
Calcium	mg	904	56	961	- 2.6	5.9
Iron	mg	11.2	0.8	11.9	- 0.8	6.4
Zinc	mg	8.3	0.7	9.0	- 0.4	7.3
Magnesium	mg	256	22	278	+ 0.2	8.0
Sodium (d)	g	2.71	0.21	2.92	- 1.8	7.2
Potassium	g	2.86	0.24	3.10	- 0.3	7.8
Thiamin	mg	1.56	0.11	1.67	- 0.3	6.7
Riboflavin	mg	1.80	0.11	1.91	- 2.9	6.0
Niacin equivalent	mg	30.7	3.3	34.0	- 0.6	9.6
Vitamin B6	mg	2.2	0.2	2.4	- 1.4	9.8
Vitamin B12	µg	5.9	0.4	6.2	- 4.1	6.0
Folate	µg	257	27	284	- 0.7	9.6
Vitamin C	mg	64	5	69	- 4.7	7.2
Vitamin A:						
Retinol	µg	470	31	500	- 8.3	6.1
β-carotene	µg	1 832	139	1 971	+ 1.6	7.0
Retinol equivalent	µg	782	54	836	- 4.3	6.4
Vitamin D	µg	2.89	0.23	3.12	- 1.4	7.4
Vitamin E	mg	10.66	1.07	11.74	- 4.6	9.1
		contributions to energy intake from food and drink excluding alcohol				
Fat	%	37.6	39.3	37.7	- 0.3	
Fatty acids:						
Saturates	%	14.8	13.7	14.8	- 0.6	
Mono-unsaturates	%	13.6	15.2	13.7	- 0.2	
Poly-unsaturates	%	6.6	7.6	6.7	- 0.1	
Carbohydrate	%	48.3	46.7	48.2	0.0	
Non-milk extrinsic sugars	%	15.0	20.8	15.5	- 1.0	
Protein	%	14.1	14.1	14.1	+ 1.0	

(a) Contributions from pharmaceutical sources are not recorded by the Survey
(b) Available carbohydrate, calculated as monosaccharide equivalent
(c) As non-starch polysaccharides
(d) Excludes sodium from table salt

Quantities of purchases

9 Table 1.2 shows estimates of quantities purchased of food and drink brought home (household purchases) and consumed outside the home (eating out purchases) in the UK in 2004-05.

10 There was an estimated reduction of 17 per cent in the quantity of household purchases of wholemilk in 2004-05. Wholemilk consumption has been in decline since 1974.

11 There was an estimated reduction of 16 per cent in the purchases of confectionery for consumption outside the home. Quantities purchased have fallen in each of the three years since 2001-02.

12 There was an estimated 5.2 per cent reduction in the quantities purchased of soft drinks for the household, but this followed a larger rise in the previous year. The quantity of soft drinks purchased for the houschold in 2004-05 was 5.1 per cent higher than in 2001-02.

13 There was an estimated 8.9 per cent reduction in the quantity of soft drinks purchased for consumption outside the home. This followed rises in the two previous years.

14 The quantity of alcoholic drinks purchased for consumption outside the home has fallen steadily each year since 2001-02. The quantity purchased was 7.3 per cent lower in 2004-05 than in 2003-04 and 16 per cent lower than in 2001-02.

15 The estimated quantities purchased of alcoholic drinks for the household was 3.7 per cent lower in 2004-05, but this followed a larger rise last year. It was estimated to be 3.8 per cent higher than in 2001-02 and is not showing the same pattern of decline as alcoholic drinks purchased for consumption outside the home. Between 1994 and 2004-05 household purchases of alcoholic drinks rose by 38 per cent.

16 The estimated quantity of purchases of fresh and processed potatoes for the household in 2004-05 was 4.9 per cent lower than in the previous year and 4.7 per cent lower for eating out. In both categories there were recorded reductions in each of the three years since 2001-02.

Table 1.2 Quantities of food purchases in the United Kingdom

		2001-02	2002-03	2003-04	2004-05	Reliability of 2004-05 estimate (b)	% change since 2003-04
Number of households in sample		7 473	6 927	7 048	6 798		
Number of persons in sample		18 122	16 586	16 965	16 257		
Household Purchases		\multicolumn{6}{c}{*grams per person per week unless otherwise stated*}
Milk and cream	ml	2 023	1 990	2 024	1 984	✓✓✓	- 2.0
Liquid whole milk	ml	599	555	585	485	✓✓	- 17.1
Cheese		112	112	113	110	✓✓✓	- 2.5
Carcase meat		229	230	225	229	✓✓✓	+ 1.0
Other meat and meat products		803	820	836	820	✓✓✓	- 2.0
Fish		157	155	156	158	✓✓✓	+ 1.1
Eggs	no.	1.65	1.66	1.62	1.56	✓✓✓	- 3.7
Fats		196	190	186	182	✓✓✓	- 2.3
Butter		41	37	35	35	✓✓	+ 0.9
Sugar and preserves		147	146	135	134	✓✓✓	- 1.0
Fresh and processed potatoes		907	873	864	822	✓✓✓	- 4.9
Fruit and vegetables excluding potatoes		2 248	2 307	2 269	2 274	✓✓✓	+ 0.2
Vegetables excluding potatoes		1 092	1 101	1 079	1 106	✓✓✓	+ 2.5
Fruit		1 156	1 206	1 190	1 168	✓✓✓	- 1.8
Fresh apples		175	172	171	173	✓✓✓	+ 1.4
Cereals		1 655	1 671	1 614	1 577	✓✓✓	- 2.2
Bread		769	757	728	695	✓✓✓	- 4.6
Beverages		60	58	55	56	✓✓✓	+ 0.3
Soft drinks (a)	ml	1 744	1 757	1 933	1 832	✓✓✓	- 5.2
Confectionery		128	127	129	131	✓✓✓	+ 1.8
Alcoholic drinks	ml	735	726	792	763	✓✓✓	- 3.7
Beers	ml	108	112	105	96	✓	- 8.4
Lagers and continental beers	ml	278	268	311	299	✓✓	- 3.8
Eating Out Purchases		\multicolumn{6}{c}{*grams per person per week unless otherwise stated*}
Indian, Chinese and Thai meals or dishes		22	22	20	21	✓	+ 6.7
Meat and meat products		94	95	97	91	✓✓✓	- 6.0
Fish and fish products		15	14	14	14	✓✓	0.0
Cheese and egg dishes and pizza		25	26	26	25	✓✓	- 4.9
Potatoes		88	85	83	79	✓✓✓	- 4.7
Vegetables		34	34	34	33	✓✓	- 0.8
Sandwiches		80	80	76	71	✓✓✓	- 7.5
Ice cream, desserts and cakes		31	32	29	29	✓✓✓	- 0.7
Beverages	ml	154	147	142	141	✓✓	- 0.8
Soft drinks including milk drinks	ml	373	376	384	350	✓✓✓	- 8.9
Confectionery		23	22	22	18	✓✓	- 16.0
Alcoholic drinks	ml	732	702	664	616	✓✓	- 7.3

(a) Converted to unconcentrated equivalent by applying a factor of 5 to concentrated and low calorie concentrated soft drinks
(b) Relative standard error. 3 ticks <2.5%, 2 ticks <5%, 1 tick < 10%, no ticks <20%

Expenditure on food and drink

17 Table 1.3 shows the estimated expenditure on food and drink in the UK in 2004-05. Overall expenditure on food and drink was estimated to have been 2.1 per cent higher in 2004-05 than in the previous year, but this was a 1.0 per cent drop in real terms. The average expenditure on all food and drink in the UK was £34.31 per person per week in 2004-05.

18 Expenditure on food and drink eaten out was 3.0 per cent higher in 2004-05 which in real terms was broadly unchanged. Expenditure on alcoholic drinks purchased for consumption outside the home was 4.7 per cent lower in real terms than in the previous year.

19 Expenditure on food and drink for the household in 2004-05 was £23.05 per person in the UK, which was 1.7 per cent higher than the previous year but 1.4 per cent lower in real terms.

Table 1.3 Expenditure on food and drink in the UK

	2001-02	2002-03	2003-04	2004-05	Reliability of 2004-05 estimate (b)	% change since 2003-04
Number of households in sample	7 473	6 927	7 048	6 798		
Number of persons in sample	18 122	16 586	16 965	16 257		
Household Expenditure				*pence per person per week unless otherwise stated*		
Milk and cream	144	147	154	156	✓✓✓	+ 1.7
Cheese	57	58	59	60	✓✓✓	+ 2.6
Carcase meat	103	106	111	114	✓✓✓	+ 2.9
Other meat and meat products	355	364	382	380	✓✓✓	- 0.6
Fish	93	93	94	99	✓✓✓	+ 5.4
Eggs	17	17	18	18	✓✓✓	+ 1.8
Fats	36	37	36	37	✓✓✓	+ 3.8
Sugar and preserves	15	16	16	17	✓✓✓	+ 6.7
Fresh and processed potatoes	104	99	102	102	✓✓✓	- 0.4
Vegetables excluding potatoes	167	170	177	182	✓✓✓	+ 2.8
Fruit	150	159	163	167	✓✓✓	+ 2.7
Cereals	357	366	368	376	✓✓✓	+ 2.1
Beverages	44	42	41	42	✓✓✓	+ 1.1
Soft drinks	72	74	83	81	✓✓✓	- 2.0
Confectionery	81	77	81	84	✓✓✓	+ 3.9
Alcoholic drinks	244	249	265	266	✓✓✓	+ 0.4
Other food	113	116	118	123	✓✓✓	+ 4.3
Household expenditure on food and non-alcoholic drink	1 908	1 942	2 002	2 039	✓✓✓	+ 1.8
Total household expenditure on food and drink	**2 152**	**2 191**	**2 267**	**2 305**	✓✓✓	**+ 1.7**
Eating Out Expenditure						
Alcoholic drinks	371	373	360	354	✓✓	- 1.7
Food and non-alcoholic drinks eaten out	698	721	733	772	✓✓✓	+ 5.3
Total expenditure on food and drink eaten out	**1 068**	**1 094**	**1 093**	**1 126**	✓✓✓	**+ 3.0**
Total expenditure on all food and drink	**3 221**	**3 285**	**3 360**	**3 431**	✓✓✓	**+ 2.3**

(a) Relative standard error. 3 ticks <2.5%, 2 ticks <5%, 1 tick < 10%, no ticks <20%

Unit values

20 Table 1.4 shows unit values or expenditure per unit quantity for various types of food and drink purchases in 2004-05. Unit values rise or fall if prices rise or fall but they also change if the pattern of purchases within a food code changes. Such a change may be towards purchases of more expensive or less expensive items within the products in a code. It may also indicate that products within a code have changed in terms of value added such as pre-packed salads or organic produce. The table also shows changes in relevant food components of the retail price index.

21 The unit value of food for the household, excluding soft drinks confectionery and alcoholic drinks, was 3.3 per cent higher in 2004-05. Compared against a corresponding food price rise of 0.3 per cent, this implies a shift of +3 per cent in value added, i.e. a shift of 3 per cent in the pattern of purchases to products of higher value.

22 For seasonal food there was a 5 per cent improvement in the value added of purchases. Fruit purchases showed the largest gain in value added with an 8 per cent rise. At the other end of the scale there were only small changes or reductions in the level of value added of purchases of various types of meat.

Table 1.4 Price and unit value changes

	Unit values from Expenditure and Food Survey				RPI	
	2002-03	2003-04	2004-05	% change into 2004-05	% change into 2004-05	% shift in value added
	pence per kg or pence per litre					
All Items Retail Price Index					1.0	
RPI food items					0.3	
Food	196	202	209	3.3	0.3	+ 3
Seasonal food	150	157	161	2.3	- 2.2	+ 5
Bread	117	123	133	8.3	3.9	+ 4
Cereals	321	330	334	1.1	0.0	+ 1
Biscuits and cakes	328	333	346	3.9	- 0.7	+ 5
Beef	485	508	520	2.3	0.9	+ 1
Lamb	500	538	528	- 2.0	2.3	- 4
Pork	403	426	439	3.0	2.2	+ 1
Bacon	527	531	528	- 0.5	0.0	0
Poultry	356	382	388	1.6	4.0	- 2
Fish	602	609	630	3.4	- 1.0	+ 4
Butter	296	293	305	4.0	3.5	0
Cheese	519	519	547	5.3	1.2	+ 4
Eggs (pence per egg)	11	11	12	6.4	4.5	+ 2
Milk	74	76	79	3.6	1.8	+ 2
Tea	523	519	511	- 1.6	- 4.9	+ 3
Coffee and hot drinks	727	742	747	0.8	- 1.2	+ 2
Soft Drinks	42	43	44	3.3	- 0.6	+ 4
Sugar and preserves	111	118	128	7.7	3.4	+ 4
Sweets and chocolates	604	629	642	2.2	3.5	- 1
Potatoes	52	56	61	8.7	2.2	+ 6
Vegetables	160	169	171	0.8	- 2.5	+ 3
Fruit	134	139	145	4.3	- 4.1	+ 8
of which fresh fruit	143	150	150	0.5	- 4.8	+ 5

Comparison with Reference Nutrient Intakes

8 Nutrient intakes derived from the survey are compared with Reference Nutrient Intakes[1]. These Reference Nutrient Intakes (RNIs) represent the best estimate of the amount of a nutrient that is enough, or more than enough, for about 97 per cent of people in a group. If average intake of a group is at the level of the RNI, then the risk of deficiency in the group is very small.

9 Energy intake is compared against the Estimated Average Requirement (EAR) for a group. Estimates of energy requirements for different populations are termed EARs and are defined as the energy intake estimated to meet the average requirements of the group. About half the people in the group will usually need more energy than the EAR and half the people in the group will usually need less.

10 Table 1.5 shows the Estimated Average Requirements for energy and the Reference Nutrient Intakes for selected nutrients for different groups of people based on their age and sex.

Table 1.5 Estimated Average Requirements for energy and Reference Nutrient Intakes for selected nutrients (a)

		Children				Males				Females				Pregnant females
Age:		Under 1	1 to 3	4 to 6	7 to 10	11 to 14	15 to 18	19 to 50	50+	11 to 14	15 to 18	19 to 50	50+	16 to 50
										reference nutrient intake per person per day				
Energy (b)	kcal	721	1 197	1 630	1 855	2 220	2 755	2 550	2 340	1 845	2 110	1 940	1 877	2 140
Protein	g	13.5	14.5	19.7	28.3	42.1	55.2	55.5	53.3	41.2	45.0	45.0	46.5	51.0
Calcium	mg	525	350	450	550	1 000	1 000	700	700	800	800	700	700	700
Iron	mg	5.4	6.9	6.1	8.7	11.3	11.3	8.7	8.7	14.8	14.8	14.8	8.7	14.8
Zinc	mg	4.5	5.0	6.5	7.0	9.0	9.5	9.5	9.5	9.0	7.0	7.0	7.0	7.0
Magnesium	mg	68	85	120	200	280	300	300	300	280	300	270	270	270
Sodium (c)	g	0.3	0.5	0.7	1.2	1.6	1.6	1.6	1.6	1.6	1.6	1.6	1.6	1.6
Potassium	g	0.8	0.8	1.1	2.0	3.1	3.5	3.5	3.5	3.1	3.5	3.5	3.5	3.5
Thiamin	mg	0.2	0.5	0.7	0.7	0.9	1.1	1.0	0.9	0.7	0.8	0.8	0.8	0.9
Riboflavin	mg	0.4	0.6	0.8	1.0	1.2	1.3	1.3	1.3	1.1	1.1	1.1	1.1	1.4
Niacin equivalent	mg	4	8	11	12	15	18	17	16	12	14	13	12	13
Vitamin B6	mg	0.3	0.7	0.9	1.0	1.2	1.5	1.4	1.4	1.0	1.2	1.2	1.2	1.2
Vitamin B12	µg	0.3	0.5	0.8	1.0	1.2	1.5	1.5	1.5	1.2	1.5	1.5	1.5	1.5
Folate	µg	50	70	100	150	200	200	200	200	200	200	200	200	300
Vitamin C	mg	25	30	30	30	35	40	40	40	35	40	40	40	50
Vitamin A (retinol equivalent)	µg	350	400	500	500	600	700	700	700	600	600	600	600	700

(a) Department of Health, Dietary Reference Values for Food Energy and Nutrients for the United Kingdom, HMSO, 1991
(b) Estimated Average Requirement
(c) The RNI for sodium is the amount that is sufficient for 97 per cent of the population. In May 2003 the Scientific Advisory Committee on Nutrition made recommendations about the maximum amount of salt that people should be eating, i.e. that the average salt intake for adults should be no more than 6 grams per day, equivalent to 2.4 grams of sodium per day.

11 To compare average intakes from food and drink against Reference Nutrient Intakes it is first necessary to obtain the average RNIs for the United Kingdom population. Table 1.6 shows the calculation of the average RNI across the UK population in 2004-05 for protein. The person count shown in the table is the number of people in the sample.

---

[1] Reference Nutrient Intakes from Department of Health, *'Dietary Reference Values for Food Energy and Nutrients for the United Kingdom'*, HMSO 1991

Table 1.6 Calculation of the UK weighted RNI for protein in 2004-05

	RNI (grams)	Person count ('000 head)	RNI x Person count
Children under 1	13.5	700	9 452
Children 1 to 3	14.5	2 006	29 084
Children 4 to 6	19.7	2 052	40 415
Children 7 to 10	28.3	2 908	82 305
Males 11 to 14	42.1	1 575	66 322
Males 15 to 18	55.2	1 636	90 282
Females 11 to 14	41.2	1 571	64 719
Females 15 to 18	45.0	1 462	65 792
Males 19 to 50	55.5	12 373	686 706
Males over 50	53.3	8 905	474 648
Females 19 to 50	45.0	12 626	568 186
Females 16 to 50 (pregnant)	51.0	413	21 081
Females over 50	46.5	10 085	468 951
Total		58 313	2 667 943

Weighted average RNI for protein = 2 667 943 / 58 313 = 45.8 grams per person.

12 An allowance of 10 per cent is made for wastage (e.g. food left on the plate) of household food and drink. In 2004-05 the average UK intake of protein from household food was 70.6 grams per person per day. Deducting 10 per cent for wastage gives an average of 63.6 grams per person per day. This is equivalent to 139 per cent of the 2004-05 weighted average RNI for protein.

13 For food and drink eaten out no allowance is made for waste. In 2004-05 the average UK intake of protein from food and drink eaten out was 5.8 grams per person per day, or 11 per cent of the 2004-05 weighted average RNI for protein.

14 For all food and drink (i.e. combining household purchases and food and drink eaten out) the average protein intake per person per day was 150 per cent of the weighted average RNI for protein in the UK in 2004-05.

Estimated intakes compared to Reference Nutrient Intakes

15 Table 1.7 shows average UK energy and nutrient intakes from food and drink per person per day as percentages of the weighted RNIs for 2004-05. When interpreting the figures it should be noted that the RNIs were set in 1991 and as life styles change these become out of date, especially in the case of energy intake. There could also be an impact due to mis-reporting of food purchases. In addition intakes from dietary supplements are not included and the figures for sodium do not include any allowance for table salt that may be added to food during cooking or before consumption.

16 Based on the food and drink purchases recorded in the Expenditure and Food Survey in 2004-05:

- Average energy intake was 96 per cent of the Estimated Average Requirement.
- Magnesium and potassium intakes were below the weighted RNI at 94 per cent and 87 per cent respectively.
- Intake of all other minerals and vitamins were above the weighted RNIs.

Table 1.7 Energy and nutrient intakes in the UK as a percentage of weighted Reference Nutrient Intakes (a)

		Nutrient intake derived from purchases			Intake as a percentage of weighted Reference Nutrient Intake (a)		
		Household	Eaten Out	Total	Household (b)	Eaten Out	Total
							per person per day
Energy (c)	kcal	2 048	191	2 239	88	8	96
Energy excluding alcohol (c)	kcal	1 996	187	2 183	86	7	93
Protein	g	70.6	5.8	76.5	139	11	150
Calcium	mg	904	56	961	118	7	125
Iron	mg	11.2	0.8	11.9	97	7	104
Zinc	mg	8.3	0.7	9.0	94	7	102
Magnesium	mg	256	22	278	87	8	94
Sodium (d)	g	2.71	0.21	2.92	163	13	176
Potassium	g	2.86	0.24	3.10	81	7	87
Thiamin	mg	1.56	0.11	1.67	167	12	179
Riboflavin	mg	1.80	0.11	1.91	142	9	151
Niacin equivalent	mg	30.7	3.3	34.0	199	21	220
Vitamin B6	mg	2.2	0.2	2.4	159	17	176
Vitamin B12	µg	5.9	0.4	6.2	381	24	406
Folate	µg	257	27	284	123	13	136
Vitamin C	mg	64	5	69	150	12	161
Vitamin A (retinol equivalent)	µg	782	54	836	113	8	121

(a) Department of Health, Dietary Reference Values for Food Energy and Nutrients for the United Kingdom, HMSO, 1991
(b) After deduction of a 10 per cent allowance for wastage
(c) Estimated Average Requirement
(d) The RNI for sodium is the amount that is sufficient for 97 per cent of the population. In May 2003 the Scientific Advisory Committee on Nutrition made recommendations about the maximum amount of salt that people should be eating, i.e. that the average salt intake for adults should be no more than 6 grams per day, equivalent to 2.4 grams of sodium per day.

Trends in estimated intakes compared to Reference Nutrient Intakes

17 Table 1.8 shows trends in the way estimated intakes compare with reference levels. Because reliable data on eating out are only available from 2001-02 intakes from eating out are not included. Though intakes of sodium are still above recommended levels there has been a gradual reduction since 2000 in the intake of sodium as a percentage of the weighted RNI.

18 Reference Nutrient Intakes from Department of Health, Dietary Reference Values for Food Energy and Nutrients for the United Kingdom, HMSO, 1991.

Table 1.8 Trends in estimated intakes compared to Reference Nutrient Intakes (a)(b)

	\multicolumn{6}{c}{Adjusted National Food Survey figures}	\multicolumn{4}{c}{Expenditure and Food Survey}
	1975	1980	1985	1990	1995	2000	2001-02	2002-03	2003-04	2004-05
									\multicolumn{2}{r}{per person per day}
Energy (c)	111	109	96	90	93	93	89	90	89	88
Energy excluding alcohol (c)					91	91	87	88	87	86
Protein	158	159	143	134	137	145	140	141	140	139
Calcium	142	134	118	115	118	127	122	122	121	118
Iron	116	111	103	99	95	100	96	97	98	97
Zinc					94	99	96	97	94	94
Magnesium					87	92	87	88	86	87
Sodium (d)			172	168	171	177	173	169	165	163
Potassium					81	86	81	81	81	81
Thiamin	137	139	153	147	157	167	160	162	167	167
Riboflavin	156	170	153	139	139	154	145	145	146	142
Niacin equivalent	205	209	186	175	182	200	196	198	199	199
Vitamin B6					158	169	160	160	161	159
Vitamin B12					337	414	382	379	397	381
Folate		116	119	127	124	130	123	124	123	123
Vitamin C	131	148	132	135	148	165	157	161	157	150
Vitamin A (retinol equivalent)	263	266	262	205	194	136	116	116	118	113

(a) Department of Health, Dietary Reference Values for Food Energy and Nutrients for the United Kingdom, HMSO, 1991
(b) After deduction of a 10 per cent allowance for wastage
(c) Estimated Average Requirement
(d) The RNI for sodium is the amount that is sufficient for 97 per cent of the population. In May 2003 the Scientific Advisory Committee on Nutrition made recommendations about the maximum amount of salt that people should be eating, i.e. that the average salt intake for adults should be no more than 6 grams per day, equivalent to 2.4 grams of sodium per day.

Chapter 2 Key Trends Informing Policy

Headlines for 2004-05

- quantities of fruit and vegetables purchased for the household show no statistically significant change since 2001-02

- average energy intake per person continues to decline; it was 1.8 per cent lower in 2004-05 than a year previously and at least 20 per cent lower than in 1974

- the percentages of food energy derived from fat and saturated fatty acids show no statistically significant change since 2001-02

- there is no trend in the percentage of food energy derived from non-milk extrinsic sugars since 2001-02

- there is a downward trend in intake of sodium, excluding sodium from table salt, since 2000

1. While many people eat well, a large number do not, particularly among the more disadvantaged and vulnerable in society. In particular, a significant proportion of the population consumes less than the recommended amount of fruit and vegetables and fibre but more than the recommended amount of fat, saturated fatty acids, salt and sugar. Such poor nutrition is a major cause of ill health and premature death. This chapter looks at key indicators of diet.

Fruit and vegetables

2. The survey estimates of quantities of purchases of fruit and vegetables are used by government to monitor trends in consumption of fruit and vegetables in support of the 5 A DAY policy to encourage people to eat more fruit and vegetables.

3. Chart 2.1 shows the quantities of household purchases of fresh and processed fruit and vegetables excluding potatoes. It shows that the level of purchases rose from the 1970s up to 1997 and then remained fairly static. In 2004-05 it was an average of 2274 grams purchased per person per week.

4. Assuming 80 grams per portion, 5 A DAY consumption for a week is 2800 grams of fruit and vegetables. Allowing ten per cent for wastage, 5 A DAY consumption requires purchases of 3080 grams per person per week. From the survey we estimated that purchases of fruit and vegetables was an average of 2274 grams per person per week. This is 74 per cent of the 5 A DAY target and equivalent to 3.7 portions per person per day after wastage. In 1974 purchases were 61 per cent of this benchmark target, equivalent to 3.0 portions per day.

5. The Department of Health takes the policy lead on public health. According to the Department of Health's 2004 Health Survey for England adults aged 16 and over consumed an average of 3.5 portions per day. For both men and women the proportion who consumed more than 5 portions per day increased between 2001 and 2004, rising from 22 per cent to 24 per cent for

Chart 2.1 Household purchases of fruit and vegetables excluding potatoes

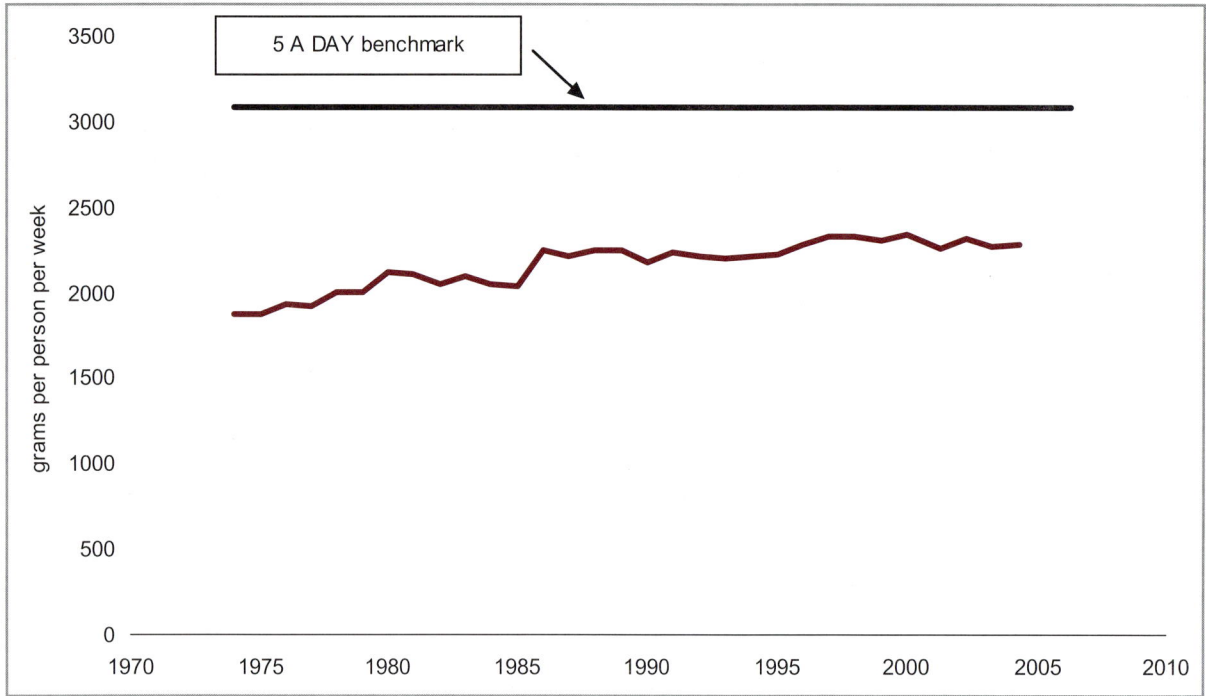

men and 25 per cent to 27 per cent for women. The 3.5 portions equates to consumption of 1941 grams per adult (16 and over) per week in England. The Expenditure and Food Survey estimate of quantities purchased in 2004-05 was 2274 grams per person per week. Allowing 10 per cent for waste gave a rough estimate of consumption as an average of 2046 grams per person per day in the UK. This estimate was 5 per cent higher than that from the Health Survey for England. This may be because the Expenditure and Food Survey estimate included all purchases of fruit juice and baked beans as opposed to the first 80 grams per person per day of each and the estimate that 10 per cent of fruit and vegetables is wasted may have been too low. The Health Survey for England estimate was for adults only whilst the Expenditure and Food Survey estimate was a population average including children. Differences in survey coverage and time period will also have had some effect.

6 Table 2.1 shows the quantity of purchases of fruit and vegetables for household supplies was almost unchanged (0.2 per cent higher) in 2004-05. None of the percentage changes from the previous year shown in the table were statistically significant. The rise in consumption since the 1970s is observable in both fresh and processed fruit but not in vegetables. In fact purchases of vegetables were estimated to be lower in 2004-05 than they were in the mid seventies.

7 Consumers are influenced by prices of produce. In 2004-05 the overall price of fruit (fresh and processed) was 4.1 per cent lower and the overall price of vegetables was 2.5 per cent lower. People spent on average £1.82 per week on vegetables excluding fresh and processed potatoes and £1.67 per week on fruit. Whilst prices were lower in 2004-05 the amount spent on fruit and vegetables was slightly higher (see also table 1.4 and chart 4.1). Given that quantities purchased hardly changed, this implies consumers purchased produce of a higher value in 2004-05 than a year previously (see also table 1.4).

Table 2.1 Quantities of household purchases of fruit and vegetables in the UK (a)

		1975	1990	2000	2001-02	2002-03	2003-04	2004-05	%change since 2003-04
		\multicolumn{8}{c}{average grams per person per week unless otherwise stated}
Fruit and vegetables excluding potatoes		1 868	2 170	2 336	2 248	2 307	2 269	2 274	+ 0.2
Fruit		738	962	1 189	1 156	1 206	1 190	1 168	- 1.8
Fresh fruit		511	624	765	750	794	789	805	+ 2.1
Processed fruit		228	338	424	406	413	401	363	- 9.6
Fruit juices (b)	ml	42	225	332	327	333	322	280	- 13.1
Fresh green vegetables		341	287	246	229	231	228	225	- 1.2
Other fresh vegetables		405	475	506	502	505	505	536	+ 6.1
Processed vegetables excluding potatoes		385	446	395	360	365	346	345	- 0.5
Fresh and processed potatoes		1 378	1 199	1 002	907	873	864	822	- 4.9

(a) adjusted National Food Survey data 1975 to 2000, Expenditure and Food Survey data 2001-02 onwards

(b) 2004-05 quantities cannot be compared with previous years due to improvements in product coding. The fall in purchased quantity may also be partly due to possible shifts in consumer preference toward fruit juice drinks

Energy intake

8 The Expenditure and Food Survey and the National Food Survey provide the best long term trends available in energy intake per person in the UK (Great Britain before 1996). These trends are important in terms of government policies to improve health. Over the long term changes in energy intake largely reflect changes in energy expenditure and therefore physical activity.

9 Chart 2.2 shows the long term trend in average energy intake per person per day. The long term trend in energy intake from food and drink is downwards. The series has gradually broadened in scope from household food excluding alcoholic drinks, soft drinks and confectionery in 1940 to all food and drink from 2001-02 onwards. However the downward trend since 1964 is visible in all components of the chart.

10 Table 2.2 shows values of the various different forms of estimate of energy intake based on the National Food Survey and the Expenditure and Food Survey. The most important changes in the surveys are highlighted but in reality smaller changes occur each year as factors used to convert purchases into intakes are periodically reviewed and updated.

11 Historical estimates of household purchases between 1974 and 2000 have been adjusted to align with the level of estimates from the Family Expenditure Survey in 2000. These estimates of household purchases are broadly comparable with estimates of household purchases from the Expenditure and Food Survey which commenced in April 2001.

12 The aligned estimates are generally higher than the original ones and indicate that the scaling has partially corrected for under-reporting in the National Food Survey. Under-reporting is likely to be lower in the Expenditure and Food Survey because it does not focus on diet but on expenditure across the board and is largely based on till receipts. However it is necessary to be aware that there is a change in methodology which makes the estimate of the year on year change unreliable between 2000 and 2001-02.

Chart 2.2 Average energy intake from food and drink since 1940

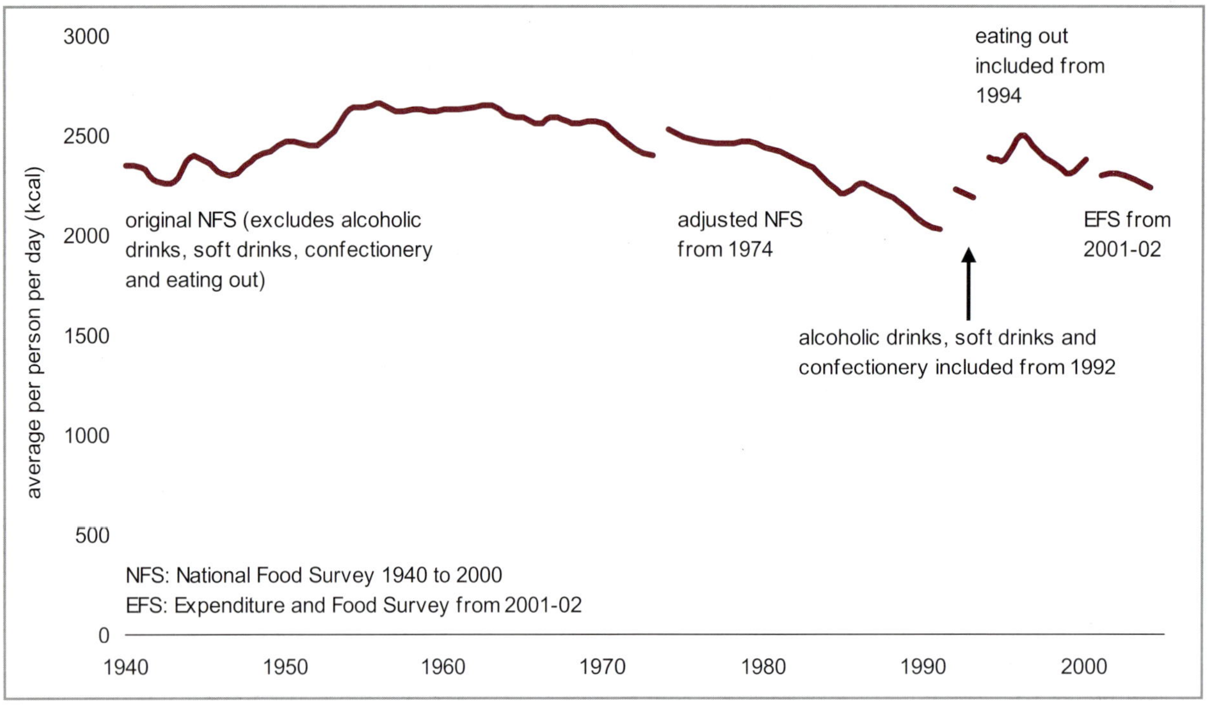

original NFS (excludes alcoholic drinks, soft drinks, confectionery and eating out)

adjusted NFS from 1974

eating out included from 1994

EFS from 2001-02

alcoholic drinks, soft drinks and confectionery included from 1992

NFS: National Food Survey 1940 to 2000
EFS: Expenditure and Food Survey from 2001-02

13 The combined series at the bottom of the table is shown because it is the best estimate for each individual year but it is not a valid time series because of the changes in definition from year to year. Combining year on year changes of estimates on like bases suggests that average energy intake per person was at least 20 per cent lower in 2004-05 than in 1974.

Table 2.2 Different estimates of energy intake as the surveys evolve

		1940	1974	1980	1990	1992	1995	2000	2001	2002	2003	2004
										kcals per person per day		
National	excluding asc (a)	2 355	2 320	2 230	1 870	1 860	1 780	1 750				
Food	Including asc (a)					1 960	1 881	1 881				
Survey	Aligned with EFS (b)		2 534	2 439	2 058	2 225	2 143	2 152				
	NFS eating out						240	230				
EFS (c)	Household								2 089	2 099	2 077	2 048
	Eating out								212	210	205	191
	Total											
Combined	Household								2 301	2 309	2 281	2 239
series (d)	Eating out											
	Total	2 355	2 534	2 439	2 058	2 225	2 143	2 152	2 089	2 099	2 077	2 048

(a) "asc" is alcoholic drinks, soft drinks and confectionery
(b) includes alcoholic drinks, soft drinks and confectionery from 1992 onwards
(c) Expenditure and Food Survey
(d) uses fullest information available each year

Fat intake and saturated fatty acid intake

14 The percentage of food energy (i.e. excluding alcohol) contributed by macronutrients is a valuable measure allowing comparisons between groups with different levels of energy expenditure and/or intake.

15 Intakes by many people of fat and, in particular, saturated fatty acids are above the 1991 recommendations of COMA. The survey provides long term trends in population average intakes based on food purchases.

16 Chart 2.3 shows that population average intakes of both fat and saturated fatty acids exceed the recommendations set in 1991 by COMA.

Chart 2.3 Intakes of fat and saturated fatty acids as a percentage of food energy intake from household supplies

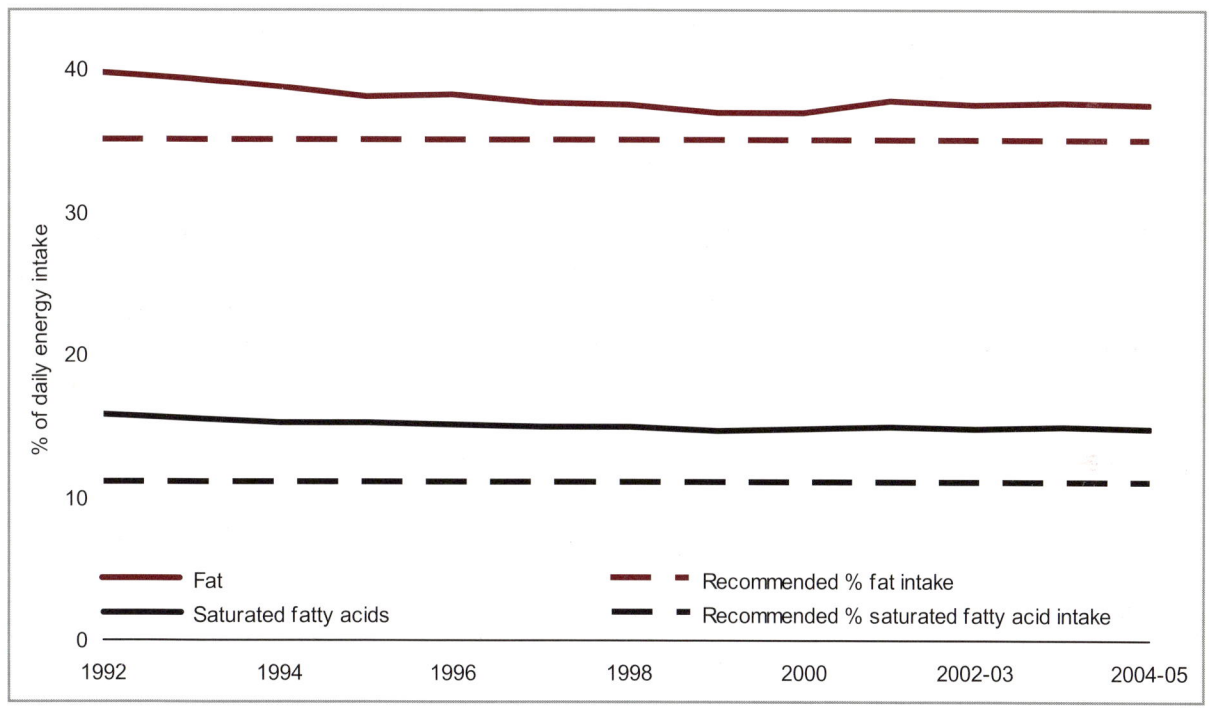

17 Table 2.3 shows that the percentage of food energy intake obtained from fat in household food has been in decline from 38.8 per cent in 1994 to 36.9 per cent in 2000. It has been relatively stable since 2001-02 and is estimated to have contributed 37.6 per cent of food energy intake in 2004-05. The recommendation is that total fat should contribute no more than 35 per cent of food energy intake for the population on average.

18 A decline is also seen in the percentage of food energy derived from saturated fatty acids in household food from 15.3 per cent in 1994 to 14.8 per cent in 2000. The percentage energy from saturated fatty acids has been relatively stable since 2001-02 and is estimated to have been 14.8 per cent in 2004-05. The recommendation is that saturated fatty acids should contribute no more than 11 per cent of food energy intake for the population on average.

19 Including the contribution of eating out purchases has little effect on the percentage contribution

Table 2.3 Percentage of food energy intake from household purchases of fat and saturated fatty acids (a)

		1994	1995	1996	1997	1998	1999	2000	2001-02	2002-03	2003-04	2004-05
		\multicolumn{11}{r}{average per person per day}
Energy intake, except from alcohol		2 101	2 103	2 200	2 126	2 060	2 012	2 101	2 041	2 051	2 025	1 998
From fat	%	38.8	38.1	38.2	37.7	37.5	37.0	36.9	37.8	37.5	37.7	37.6
From saturated fatty acids	%	15.3	15.2	15.1	15.0	15.0	14.7	14.8	14.9	14.8	14.9	14.8

(a) adjusted National Food Survey data 1994 to 2000, Expenditure and Food Survey data 2001-02 onwards

of fat and saturated fatty acids to energy intakes. In 2004-05 taking household and eating out purchases together the percentage of food energy intake from fat is 37.7 per cent and from saturated fatty acids 14.8 per cent.

Non-milk extrinsic sugars

20 The percentage of food energy (i.e. excluding alcohol) contributed by the various macronutrients is a valuable measure allowing comparisons between groups with different levels of energy expenditure and/or intake.

21 Intakes by many people of non-milk extrinsic sugars are above the 1991 recommendations of COMA. The survey provides long term trends in intakes derived from food purchases

22 Chart 2.4 shows that the percentage of food energy obtained from non-milk extrinsic sugars (mainly the sugars added during processing or at the table) in household supplies has been relatively stable since 1994. The recommendation is that non-milk extrinsic sugars should

Chart 2.4 Average daily intake from household supplies of sodium and per cent of food energy derived from non-milk extrinsic sugars, with recommended levels

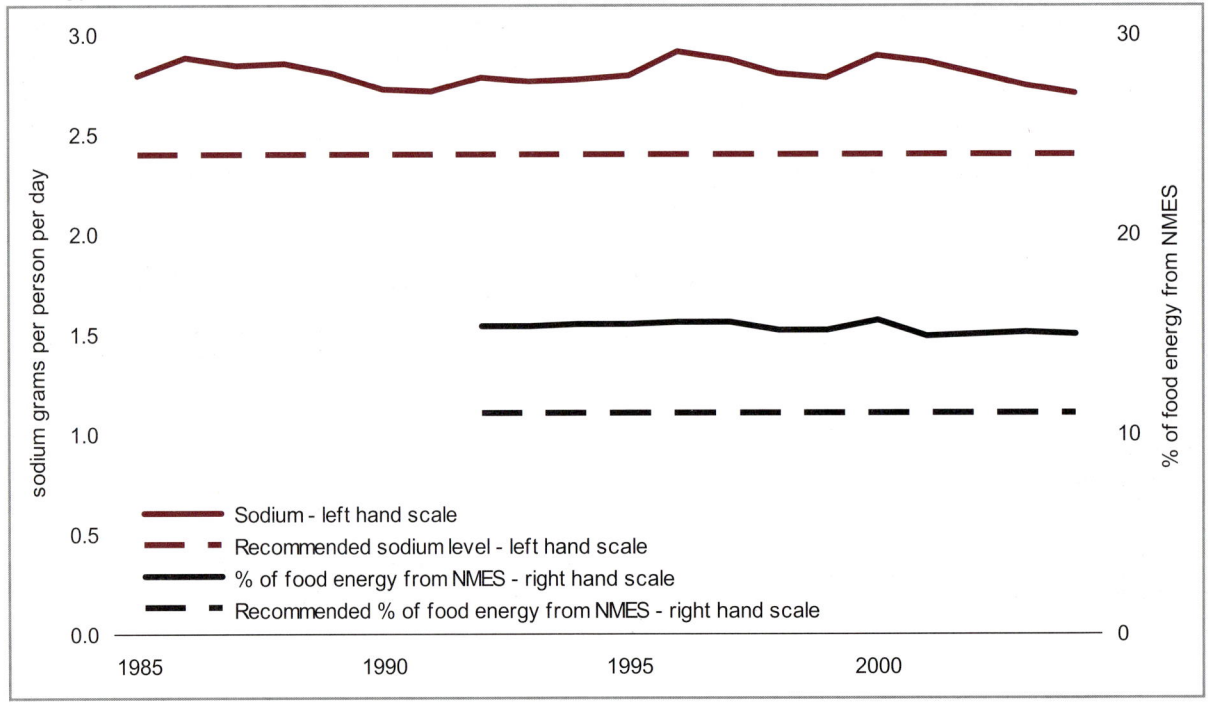

contribute no more than 11 per cent of food energy intake for the population on average. In 2004-05 15.0 per cent of food energy intake from household food was derived from non-milk extrinsic sugars, exceeding the recommendation (table 2.4). For eating out the percentage was 20.8 per cent.

Sodium

23 Chart 2.4 also shows that the intake of sodium based on household food purchases has remained stable since 1985, the earliest year for which data are available.

24 However, there is a downward trend since 2000 in intake of sodium from household supplies, excluding sodium from table salt. However intake of sodium in 2004-05, even when excluding sodium from table salt, was above the maximum recommendations made in 1991 by COMA. The Heath Survey for England, run by the Department of Health, provides more complete results on sodium intakes since it measures sodium levels directly rather than based on food purchases.

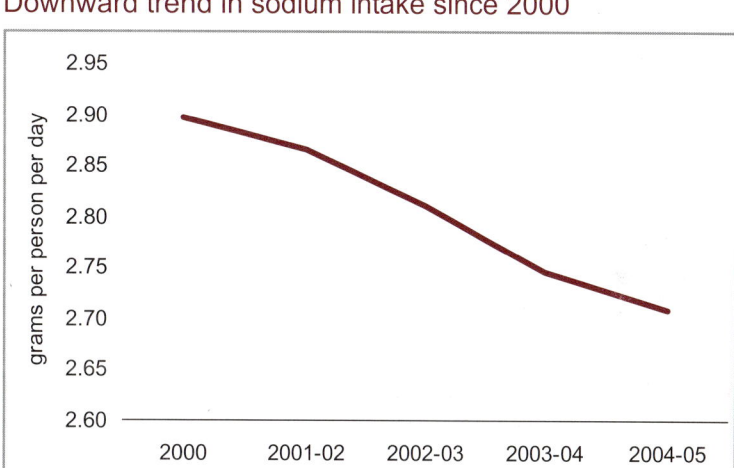

Downward trend in sodium intake since 2000

25 Sodium from table salt is excluded because purchases of table salt are not closely related to consumption. The estimate of sodium intake for 2004-05 is an average of 2.71 grams per person per day (table 2.4). It reduces to an average of 2.44 grams per person per day after allowing ten per cent for wastage. In the report on Nutritional Aspects of Cardiovascular Disease, the Committee on Medical Aspects of Food Policy (COMA) recommended an intake of salt of 6 grams per day or less for adults. This is equivalent to an intake of 2.4 grams of sodium per day. This recommendation was endorsed by the Scientific Advisory Committee on Nutrition in its recent report Salt and Health. Despite excluding sodium from table salt and sodium from food eaten out, this estimate of population average intake of sodium exceeded the recommendation.

Table 2.4 Intake of non-milk extrinsic sugars and intake of sodium from household purchases (a)

		1994	1995	1996	1997	1998	1999	2000	2001-02	2002-03	2003-04	2004-05
										average per person per day		
Energy intake, except from alcohol	kcal	2 101	2 103	2 200	2 126	2 060	2 012	2 101	2 041	2 051	2 025	1 998
Energy intake from non-milk extrinsic sugars	%	15.5	15.5	15.6	15.6	15.2	15.2	15.7	14.9	15.0	15.1	15.0
Sodium intake, except from table salt	mg	2 777	2 798	2 924	2 880	2 811	2 786	2 896	2 867	2 811	2 747	2 709

(a) adjusted National Food Survey data 1994 to 2000, Expenditure and Food Survey data 2001-02 onwards

Chapter 3 Trends in Household Purchases

Headlines

In 2004-05, compared with 2003-04, UK household purchases of

- whole milk fell by 17 per cent
- skimmed milks rose by 4.9 per cent
- yoghurts and fromage frais rose by 6.1 per cent
- cooked bacon and ham fell by 8.5 per cent
- fresh potatoes fell by 5.0 per cent
- other fresh vegetables rose by 6.1 per cent
- frozen vegetables fell by 12 per cent
- wholemeal bread rose by 18 per cent
- white bread fell by 14 per cent
- soft drinks fell by 5.2 per cent
- alcoholic drinks fell by 3.7 per cent

Other changes shown in the tables below may be due to sampling error or changes in the way the coding is performed.

1. This section presents trends in quantities of purchases of food and drink for household supplies, which includes all food and drink brought into the household. Eating out purchases are covered in chapter 6. The weights and volumes of food and drink apply to when they enter the household.

2. Purchases differ from actual food and drink consumption for a number of reasons e.g. food may be discarded during food preparation (e.g. vegetable peelings), food may be left on the plate at the end of a meal or food may become inedible before it can be consumed and is therefore thrown away. Food purchased by the household may also be consumed by visitors to the house. Purchases are recorded in the form in which they are bought. For example purchases of flour, fat, eggs and sugar are recorded as such, even if they are later used to bake a cake. If a ready-made cake is bought then it is recorded as cake.

3. Throughout the chapter figures used prior to 2001-02 are adjusted National Food Survey estimates. The adjustments brought the results of the National Food Survey into line with the Expenditure and Food Survey, and tended to increase estimates of food and drink purchases. The largest adjustments were for confectionery, alcoholic drinks, beverages and sugar and preserves. Adjustments for eggs and carcase meat resulted in reduced National Food Survey estimates. Details of the adjustments to the National Food Survey estimates can be found in Family Food 2002-03.

[4] More detailed series for 1974 to 2004-05 can be found on the Defra website. For trends in UK household consumption the most appropriate dataset to use is: http://statistics.defra.gov.uk/esg/publications/efs/datasets/efscons.xls

Milk, cream and cheese

[5] Household purchases of milk and cream in 2004-05 were 2.0 per cent lower than in the previous year (see table 3.1). Semi-skimmed milk accounted for 60 per cent of liquid milk purchases, whole milk accounted for 30 per cent and fully-skimmed milk for the remaining 10 per cent. There was a 17 per cent fall in purchases of liquid whole milk.

[6] Chart 3.1 shows trends in household purchases of drinking milk from 1974 to 2004-05. Total household purchases of drinking milk fell by 40 per cent between 1974 and 2004-05. In 2004-5 purchases of skimmed and semi-skimmed milks dominated the market, whilst in 1974 purchases of anything other than whole milk were rare.

[7] Purchases of yoghurt and fromage frais in 2004-05 were 6.1 per cent higher than in 2003-04 at 187 grams per person per week. In 1974 purchases of yoghurt and fromage frais were only 33 grams per person per week.

[8] Total cheese purchases were slightly lower in 2004-05.

Table 3.1 UK household purchases of milk, cream and cheese

		1974	1994	1999	2003-04	2004-05	Reliability of 2004-05 estimate (a)	% change since 2003-04
		millilitres per person per week unless otherwise stated
Total milk and cream		2 978	2 265	2 086	2 024	1 984	✓✓✓	- 2.0
Liquid wholemilk		2 687	877	646	585	485	✓✓	- 17.1
Skimmed milks:		5	1 092	1 150	1 081	1 133	✓✓✓	+ 4.9
Fully-skimmed		2	212	168	154	158	✓✓	+ 2.3
Semi and other skimmed		3	880	982	926	975	✓✓✓	+ 5.3
Other milks and dairy desserts (b)	eq. ml	238	137	120	162	159	-	- 1.7
Yoghurt and fromage frais		33	138	149	177	187	✓✓✓	+ 6.1
Cream		15	21	20	20	19	✓✓	- 4.1
Total cheese	g	105	106	103	113	110	✓✓✓	- 2.5
Natural cheese	g	97	96	93	99	96	✓✓✓	- 2.8
Processed cheese	g	8	10	10	14	14	✓✓	- 0.3

(a) Relative standard error. 3 ticks <2.5%, 2 ticks <5%, 1 tick < 10%, no ticks <20%, 1 cross >20%, - not available
(b) Includes condensed, infant and instant milks

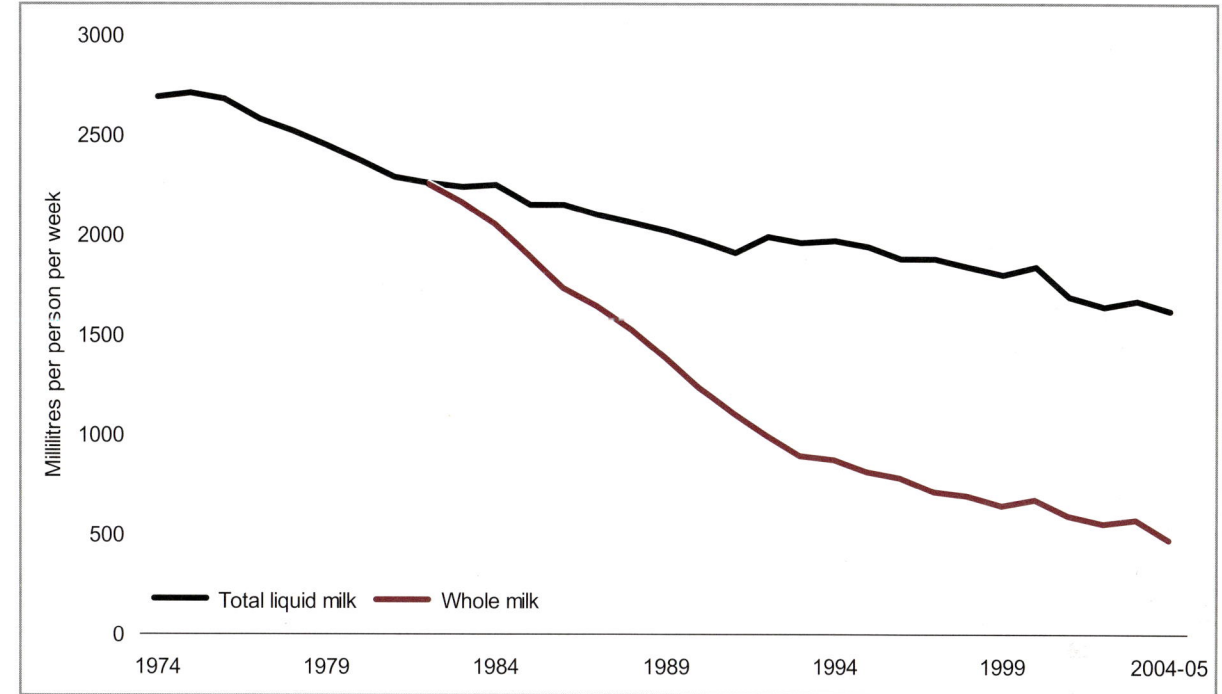

Chart 3.1 UK household liquid milk purchases 1974 to 2004-05

Meat, fish and eggs

9 In 2004-05 purchases of non-carcase meat fell by 2.0 per cent, offsetting a 1.9 per cent rise in carcase meat consumption and resulting in an overall fall of 1.2 per cent in purchases of total meat and meat products. Beef and veal carcase meat purchases rose by 3.5 per cent, while there was little change in pork, mutton and lamb. In the non-carcase meat sector there was a

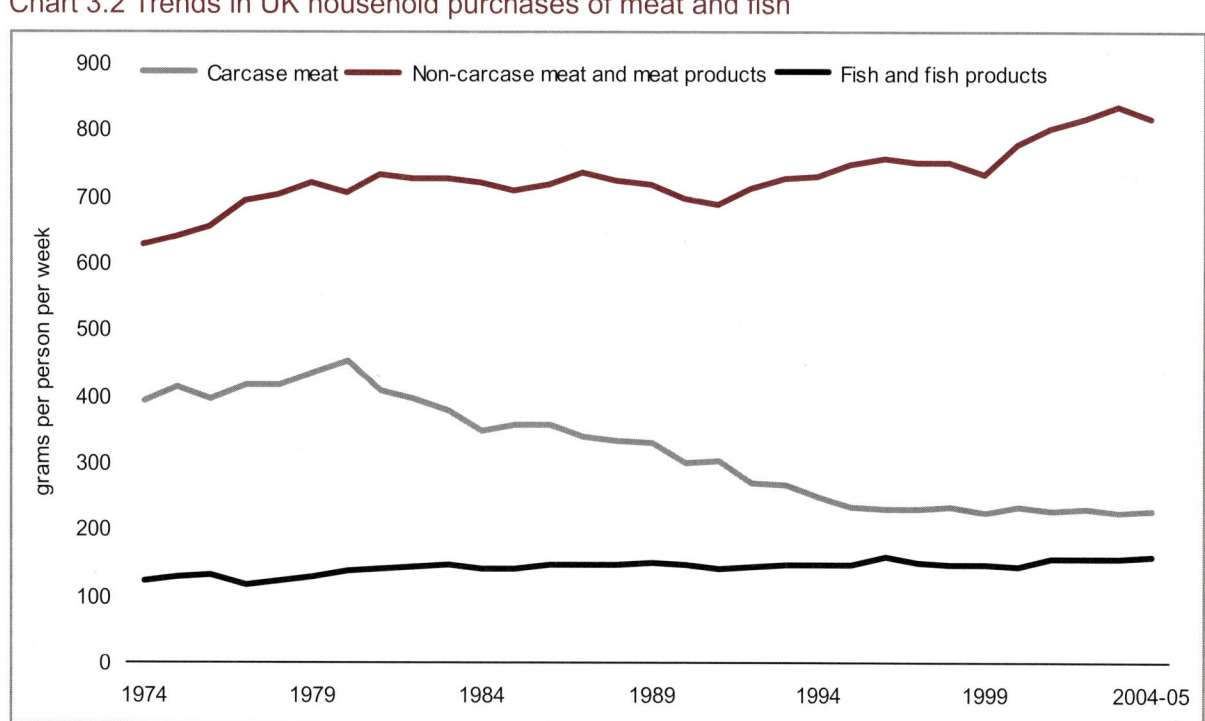

Chart 3.2 Trends in UK household purchases of meat and fish

fall of 8.5 per cent in purchases of cooked bacon and ham.

10 From 1974 household purchases of carcase meat gradually declined until 1995, but have been fairly steady since then. For non-carcase meats increasing purchases of poultry meat and ready-meals account for most of the upward trend seen since 1974.

11 There was another modest increase in purchases of fish in 2004-05 compared with the previous year. Fish ready meals showed a 2.6 per cent increase from 43 to 45 grams per person per week. Since 1974 household purchases of fish have increased by 28 per cent.

12 The average number of eggs purchased per person per week in 2004-05 was similar to the previous year. Since 1974 household purchases of eggs have fallen by 58 per cent from 3.7 eggs per person per week to 1.6 eggs per person per week in 2004-05.

13 Chart 3.2 illustrates the long-term trends in household purchases of meat and fish.

Table 3.2 Trends in UK household purchases of meat, fish and eggs

	1974	1994	1999	2003-04	2004-05	Reliability of 2004-05 estimate (a)	% change since 2003-04
						grams per person per week unless otherwise stated	
Total meat and meat products	1 023	981	961	1 061	1 049	✓✓✓	- 1.2
Carcase	393	250	226	225	229	✓✓✓	+ 1.9
Beef and veal	189	118	101	119	123	✓✓✓	+ 3.5
Mutton and lamb	113	54	56	49	50	✓	+ 1.0
Pork	91	77	69	56	56	✓✓	- 0.5
Non-carcase	630	732	735	836	820	✓✓✓	- 2.0
Bacon and ham, uncooked	116	75	66	70	70	✓✓✓	+ 0.4
Bacon and ham, cooked (b)	25	36	37	47	43	✓✓✓	- 8.5
Poultry, uncooked	127	188	180	200	197	-	- 1.4
Poultry, cooked (b)	5	19	41	48	49	✓✓	+ 1.9
Ready meals and convenience meat products	27	104	129	155	155	✓✓✓	+ 0.3
Other	329	310	282	316	305	-	- 3.6
Total fish	123	148	146	156	158	✓✓✓	+ 1.1
White, fresh chilled and frozen	44	37	33	27	26	✓	- 4.1
Herrings and other blue fish, fresh chilled and frozen	3	3	6	8	6	✓	- 20.5
Salmon, fresh chilled and frozen	2	5	8	10	10	✓	+ 0.3
Blue fish, dried salted and smoked	6	5	4	5	6	✓	+ 10.9
White fish, dried salted and smoked	5	5	6	4	4	✓	+ 6.1
Shellfish	2	5	5	11	11	✓✓	+ 1.7
Takeaway fish	20	18	11	11	11	✓✓	+ 8.1
Salmon, canned	6	9	5	6	6	✓	- 0.7
Other canned or bottled fish	12	23	27	28	30	✓✓	+ 5.4
Ready meals	23	35	26	43	45	✓✓✓	+ 2.6
Takeaway fish meals	2	4	14	2	2	✓	- 0.7
Eggs no.	3.7	1.7	1.5	1.6	1.6	✓✓✓	- 3.7

(a) Relative standard error. 3 ticks <2.5%, 2 ticks <5%, 1 tick < 10%, no ticks <20%, 1 cross >20%, - not available
(b) Excludes canned

Fats

14 Total purchases of fats and oils were 2.3 per cent lower in 2004-05 than in 2003-04 (see table 3.3).

15 Since 1974 purchases of butter, margarine and other fats (including lard) have to a large extent been replaced by purchases of low fat spreads, reduced fat spreads and vegetable and salad oils. Butter purchases fell by 43 per cent from the level in 1974, and margarine purchases fell by 76 per cent. Purchases of low fat and reduced fat spreads increased from negligible quantities in 1974 to an average of 68 grams per person per week in 2004-05.

Table 3.3 UK household purchases of fats and oils

		1974	1994	1999	2003-04	2004-05	Reliability of 2004-05 estimate (a)	% change since 2003-04
					grams per person per week unless otherwise stated
Total fats and oils		316	235	192	186	182	✓✓✓	- 2.3
Butter		147	36	35	35	35	✓✓	+ 0.9
Margarine		78	46	20	12	11	✓	- 13.0
Low fat and reduced fat spreads		1	77	74	71	68	-	- 4.4
Reduced fat spreads		0	51	51	58	44	✓✓✓	- 23.7
Low fat spreads		1	26	22	13	23	✓✓	+ 82.9
Vegetable and salad oils	ml	22	52	49	55	55	✓✓	+ 1.1
Other fats and oils (including lard)		66	24	14	13	13	-	- 4.3

(a) Relative standard error. 3 ticks <2.5%, 2 ticks <5%, 1 tick < 10%, no ticks <20%, 1 cross >20%, - not available

Sugar and preserves

16 Household purchases of sugar and preserves were 1.0 per cent lower in 2004-05 than in 2003-04 (see table 3.4). Purchases of sugar in 2004-05 were 78 per cent lower than in 1974 and purchases of honey, preserves, syrup and treacle were 55 per cent lower.

Table 3.4 UK household purchases of sugar and preserves

	1974	1994	1999	2003-04	2004-05	Reliability of 2004-05 estimate (a)	% change since 2003-04
						grams per person per week
Total sugar and preserves	316	235	192	186	182	✓✓✓	- 1.0
Sugar	147	36	35	35	35	✓✓	- 3.1
Honey, preserves, syrup and treacle	78	46	20	12	11	✓✓	+ 5.3

(a) Relative standard error. 3 ticks <2.5%, 2 ticks <5%, 1 tick < 10%, no ticks <20%, 1 cross >20%, - not available

Fruit and vegetables

17 Fresh potato purchases were 5.0 per cent lower in 2004-05 than in the previous year, and purchases of processed potato products were 4.6 per cent lower (see table 3.5). Purchases of fresh potatoes were 57 per cent lower in 2004-05 than in 1974. Purchases of processed potatoes more than doubled over the same period.

18 Total vegetable consumption excluding fresh and processed potatoes was 2.5 per cent higher in 2004-05 than in 2003-04 at 1106 grams per person per week. Fresh green vegetable purchases were 1.2 per cent lower at 225 grams per person per week, whilst other fresh vegetable purchases increased by 6.1 per cent to 536 grams per person per week. Purchases of frozen vegetables fell by 12 per cent to 66 grams per person per week. Purchases of other vegetables (mainly processed tomatoes, peas and beans and vegetable ready meals) were 2.8 per cent higher at 279 grams per person per week.

19 In 2004-05 vegetable purchases (excluding fresh and processed potatoes) were 3.1 per cent lower than in 1974. Purchases of fresh green vegetables were 38 per cent lower but purchases of other fresh vegetables were 32 per cent higher. Purchases of frozen vegetables and canned, bottled, dried and other processed vegetables declined over the same period. Chart 3.3 shows the long term trends in purchases of fresh and processed potatoes, fresh vegetables, frozen vegetables and other vegetable products

Table 3.5 UK household purchases of fruit and vegetables

	1974	1994	1999	2003-04	2004-05	Reliability of 2004-05 estimate (a)	% change since 2003-04
	grams per person per week unless otherwise stated						
Total vegetables including potatoes	2 578	2 245	2 137	1 943	1 927	✓✓✓	- 0.8
Fresh potatoes	1 318	820	693	600	570	✓✓✓	- 5.0
Processed potatoes	119	265	278	264	252	✓✓✓	- 4.6
Total vegetables excluding potatoes	1 141	1 161	1 166	1 079	1 106	✓✓✓	+ 2.5
Fresh green vegetables	364	254	251	228	225	✓✓✓	- 1.2
Fresh cabbages	129	67	54	43	45	✓✓	+ 4.6
Fresh cauliflowers	87	89	84	76	72	✓✓✓	- 4.8
Other fresh vegetables	404	480	513	505	536	✓✓✓	+ 6.1
Fresh carrots	87	118	115	99	104	✓✓✓	+ 4.9
Onions, leeks and shallots	87	94	98	96	102	✓✓	+ 6.5
Fresh tomatoes	106	94	103	98	99	✓✓✓	+ 1.2
Miscellaneous other fresh vegetables	24	54	71	90	99	✓✓	+ 10.3
All frozen vegetables (b)	72	121	99	75	66	✓✓	- 12.4
Other vegetables, not frozen (c)	300	306	303	271	279	-	+ 2.8
Total fruit	731	1 039	1 131	1 190	1 168	✓✓✓	- 1.8
Fresh fruit	515	665	729	789	805	✓✓✓	+ 2.1
Fresh apples	207	186	174	171	173	✓✓✓	+ 1.4
Fresh bananas	84	169	210	211	217	✓✓✓	+ 2.9
Fruit juices (d) ml	34	267	315	322	280	✓✓✓	- 13.1
Other fruit products	182	106	87	80	83	-	+ 4.6

(a) Relative standard error. 3 ticks <2.5%, 2 ticks <5%, 1 tick < 10%, no ticks <20%, 1 cross >20%, - not available
(b) Excludes potato products
(c) Mainly processed tomatoes, peas and beans and ready meals
(d) 2004-05 quantities cannot be compared with previous years due to improvements in product coding. The fall in purchased quantity may also be partly due to possible shifts in consumer preference toward fruit juice drinks

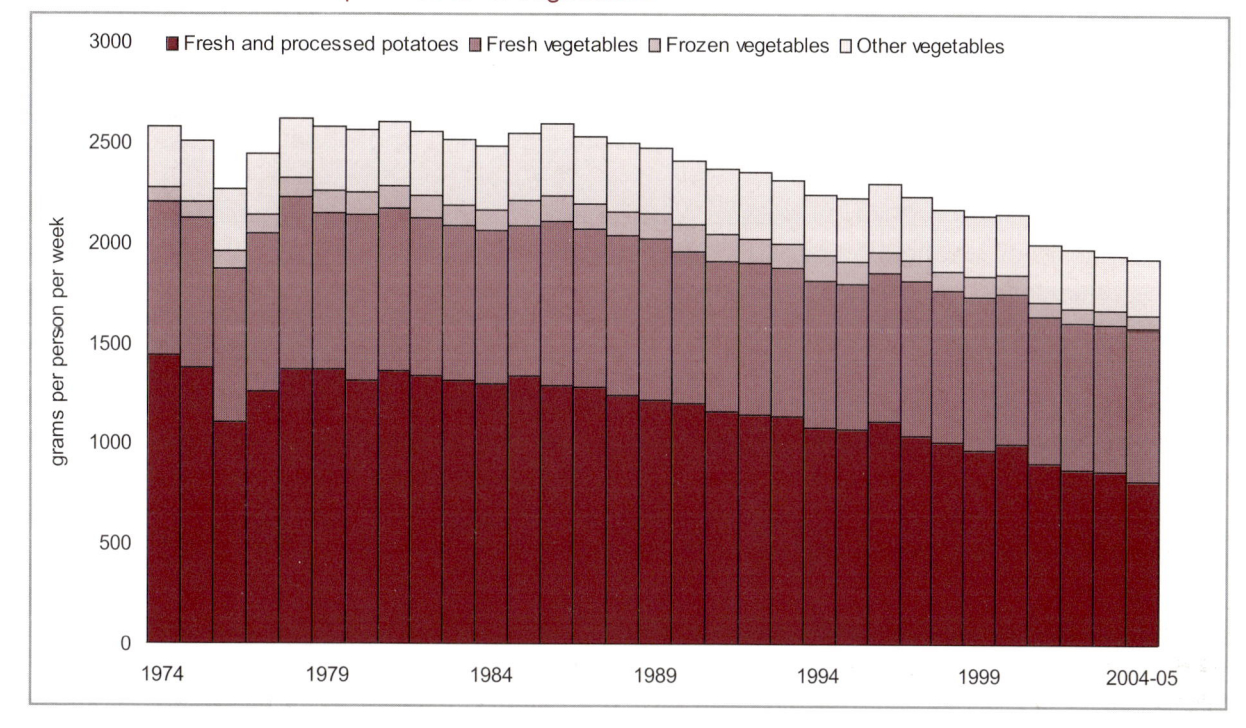

Chart 3.3 UK household purchases of vegetables

20 In 2004-05 household purchases of fresh fruit were 2.1 per cent higher than in the previous year. The figures for fruit juice cannot be compared directly with figures for recent years. During 2004-05 the procedures for coding pure fruit juice, fruit drinks and other soft drinks were improved. Fewer drinks were classified as pure fruit juice as a result of these changes.

21 Total fruit purchases were 60 per cent higher in comparison with 1974. Fresh fruit purchases rose by 56 per cent over the same period. Fruit juice purchases in 2004-05 were seven times greater than in 1974.

22 The following chart shows how the types of fresh fruit being purchased have changed between 1974 and 2004-05. In 1974 apples, pears and citrus fruits accounted for about three-quarters of fresh fruit purchases. In 2004-05 these fruits account for less than half of the fresh fruit purchases. Purchases of bananas, stone fruits and soft fruits have all increased.

Chart 3.4 Comparison of fresh fruit purchases in 1974 and 2004-05

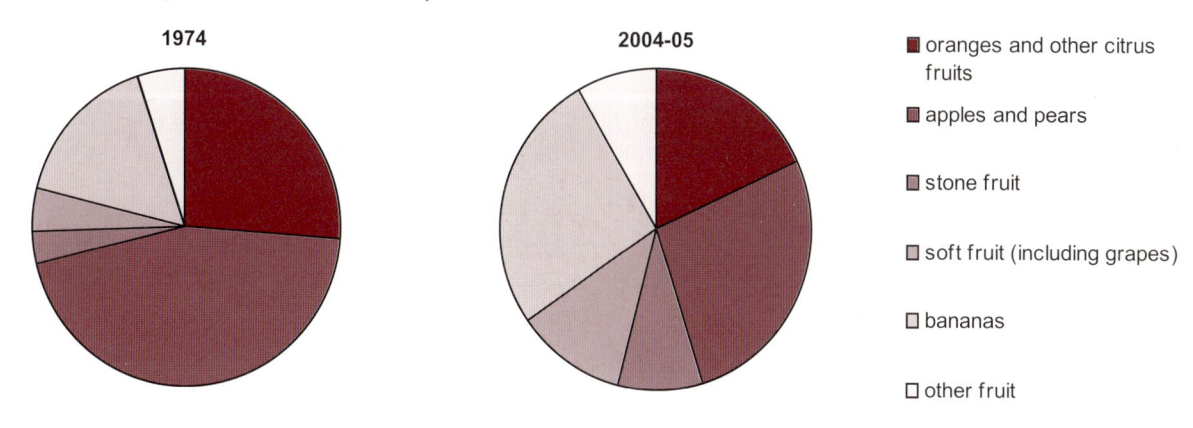

Total purchases = 515 g per person per week   Total purchases = 805 g per person per week

Bread, cereals and cereal products

23 Household purchases of bread were 4.6 per cent lower in 2004-05 in comparison with 2003-04, at an average of 695 grams per person per week (see table 3.6). Purchases of white bread, rolls, sandwiches and other breads were all lower but brown and wholemeal breads were higher.

24 Between 1974 and 2004-05 household bread purchases fell by 31.8 per cent. White bread purchases fell by about 59 per cent and brown bread purchases fell by about 31 per cent over the same period. Wholemeal bread purchases on the other hand were more than six times higher in 2004-05 than in 1974.

25 There was little change in household purchases of cereals and cereals products in 2004-05. There were slight increases in household purchases of flour, buns, scones and tea-cakes, biscuits, oatmeal and pizza and small decreases in purchases of cakes and pastries, breakfast cereals, rice, pasta and other cereals. Since 1974 the largest increases in household purchases have been in rice, pasta, pizza and breakfast cereals.

Table 3.6 UK household purchases of bread, cereals and cereal products

	1974	1994	1999	2003-04	2004-05	Reliability of 2004-05 estimate (a)	% change since 2003-04
						grams per person per week	
Total cereals including bread	1 842	1 620	1 641	1 614	1 577	✓✓✓	- 2.2
Bread	1 019	820	779	728	695	✓✓✓	- 4.6
White bread	860	472	450	410	353	✓✓✓	- 13.9
Brown bread	65	90	75	38	45	✓✓	+ 17.2
Wholemeal bread	17	112	95	101	120	✓✓✓	+ 18.2
Rolls and sandwiches	56	87	83	86	85	-	- 0.6
Other bread	21	59	76	93	92	-	- 0.9
Cereals excluding bread	823	800	861	885	882	✓✓✓	- 0.3
Flour	162	65	58	52	55	✓	+ 5.2
Cakes and pastries	158	157	152	133	126	-	- 5.0
Buns, scones and tea-cakes	30	42	45	44	47	✓✓✓	+ 7.0
Biscuits	214	184	177	163	165	✓✓✓	+ 1.1
Oatmeal and oat products	13	10	12	12	14	✓	+ 15.2
Breakfast cereals	77	126	126	134	131	✓✓✓	- 2.4
Rice	17	41	74	80	79	✓	- 1.6
Pasta	31	33	64	83	81	✓✓✓	- 1.9
Pizza	0	38	62	67	69	✓✓✓	+ 2.3
Other cereals	121	105	92	117	116	-	- 1.1

(a) Relative standard error. 3 ticks <2.5%, 2 ticks <5%, 1 tick < 10%, no ticks <20%, 1 cross >20%, - not available

Beverages and miscellaneous foods

26 There was little change in household purchases of beverages in 2004-05 in comparison to 2003-04, at an average of 56 grams per person per week (see table 3.7). Since 1974 purchases of beverages have fallen by almost 50 per cent.

27 There was little change in purchases of miscellaneous foods and drinks in 2004-05. The fall of 8.7 per cent in purchases of ice cream and related products was offset by a rise of 6.2 per cent in mineral water purchases. Mineral waters, ice cream and ice cream products show the largest increases in purchases between 1974 and 2004-05.

Table 3.7 UK household purchases of beverages and miscellaneous foods and drinks

		1974	1994	1999	2003-04	2004-05	Reliability of 2004-05 estimate (a)	% change since 2003-04
		grams per person per week unless otherwise stated
Total beverages		107	75	68	55	56	✓✓✓	+ 0.3
Tea		68	41	35	31	31	✓✓✓	+ 1.6
Coffee		20	18	16	17	17	-	+ 0.5
Cocoa and drinking chocolate		10	6	9	4	4	✓	- 7.3
Branded food drinks		9	10	9	4	4	✓	- 2.8
Total miscellaneous		291	462	529	697	696	✓✓✓	- 0.2
Mineral water	ml	0	125	184	236	251	✓✓	+ 6.2
Soups		105	72	72	81	81	-	+ 0.2
Pickles and sauces		52	91	107	121	120	✓✓✓	- 0.9
Ice-cream and ice-cream products	ml	44	123	114	194	177	✓✓	- 8.7
Other foods (b)		90	50	53	66	68	-	+ 2.8

(a) Relative standard error. 3 ticks <2.5%, 2 ticks <5%, 1 tick < 10%, no ticks <20%, 1 cross >20%, - not available

Soft and alcoholic drinks and confectionery

28 In line with the rest of this chapter the figures shown in table 3.8 are for purchases of drinks and confectionery for household supplies, which includes all food and drink brought into the household. Eating out purchases are covered in chapter 6. Soft drinks, alcoholic drinks and confectionery were not part of the National Food Survey in 1974, so figures are only shown for 1994 onwards in table 3.8.

29 In 2004-05 household purchases of soft drinks were 5.2 per cent lower than in 2003-04. This excludes purchases of fruit juices as they are included in the survey as fruit products (see table 3.5). Between 1994 and 2004-05 household purchases of soft drinks rose by over 20 per cent.

30 Household purchases of alcoholic drinks were 3.7 per cent lower in 2004-05 than in 2003-04 with falling purchases in all categories. Between 1994 and 2004-05 household purchases of alcoholic drinks rose by 38 per cent.

31 Household purchases of confectionery were 1.8 per cent higher in 2004-05 with only purchases of mints and boiled sweets showing a fall. Between 1994 and 2004-05 household purchases of confectionery rose by 9.4 per cent.

Table 3.8 UK household purchases of soft and alcoholic drinks and confectionary

	1994	1999	2003-04	2004-05	Reliability of 2004-05 estimate (a)	% change since 2003-04
					millilitres per person per week	
Total soft drinks (b) (c)	1 513	1 584	1 933	1 832	✓✓✓	- 5.2
Concentrated (c)	613	600	660	626	✓✓	- 5.3
Ready to drink	484	502	762	765	✓✓✓	+ 0.4
Low-calorie, concentrated (c)	197	191	148	135	✓	- 8.8
Low-calorie, ready to drink	220	292	362	306	✓✓	- 15.4
Total alcoholic drinks (average for whole population)	552	640	792	763	✓✓✓	- 3.7
Beer (d)	122	113	105	96	✓	- 8.4
Lager and continental beer (d)	189	216	311	299	✓✓	- 3.8
Wine	144	197	237	249	✓✓	+ 5.2
Other (e)	98	114	139	118	-	- 14.9
Estimated average alcoholic drink purchases by people aged 14 or over						
Total	-	-	958	921	-	- 3.8
Beer (d)	-	-	127	116	-	- 8.5
Lager and continental beer (d)	-	-	376	361	-	- 4.0
Wine	-	-	287	301	-	+ 5.0
Other (e)	-	-	168	143	-	- 15.1
					grams per person per week	
Total confectionery	120	126	129	131	✓✓✓	+ 1.8
Solid chocolate	26	26	27	30	✓✓	+ 9.3
Chocolate coated bars/sweets	57	63	59	60	✓✓	+ 1.5
Mints and boiled sweets	31	30	37	35	✓✓	- 3.7
Other	6	7	6	7	-	+ 3.7

(a) Relative standard error. 3 ticks <2.5%, 2 ticks <5%, 1 tick < 10%, no ticks <20%, 1 cross >20%, - not available
(b) Excluding pure fruit juices which are recorded in the survey under fruit products
(c) Converted to unconcentrated equivalent
(d) Including low alcohol lager and beers
(e) Including ciders, perrys, fortified wines, spirits, liqueurs and alcoholic carbonates
 - Not available

Takeaway foods brought home

32 Takeaway foods brought home are meals brought home that are ready to eat without cooking or heating. The items have already been covered in previous tables in this chapter, e.g. meat pies and pasties in table 3.2. A small number of items may be missed out of this section because they are not clearly identifiable as takeaway foods on the respondents diaries. The amounts are generally small because they are shown as averages over the whole population but many people don't make such purchases.

33 There was little change in UK takeaway food purchases in 2004-05. Meat based meals (e.g. Indian and Chinese takeaways), chips, rice and pizza accounted for most of the purchases (see table 3.9).

34 Purchases of takeaway meat based meals, rice and pizza rose considerably between 1974 and 2004-05, while sales of takeaway fish fell.

Table 3.9 UK takeaway food purchases brought home (a)

	1974	1994	1999	2002-03	2003-04	2004-05	Reliability of 2004-05 estimate (b)
							grams per person per week
Total Meat	17	62	82	65	65	66	-
Chicken	1	2	12	6	5	6	✓
Meat pies and pasties	2	5	6	4	3	3	✓
Burger and bun	1	6	7	6	6	6	✓
Kebabs	2	6	7	9	9	9	✓
Sausages and saveloys	0	2	2	3	3	3	✓
Meat based meals	11	41	48	38	40	39	✓✓
Miscellaneous meats	0	0	1	0	0	0	x
Total Fish	22	22	26	14	13	14	-
Fish	20	18	11	11	11	11	✓✓
Fish products	0	1	1	1	1	1	
Fish based meals	2	3	13	2	2	2	✓
Total Vegetables	50	56	49	57	57	58	-
Chips	48	45	39	48	46	46	✓✓
Vegetable takeaway products	2	11	11	9	10	11	✓
Total Bread	-	-	-	5	5	5	-
Sandwiches	1	2	3	3	3	3	✓
Breads	-	-	-	2	2	2	✓
Total Other cereals	-	-	-	41	42	44	-
Pastries	-	-	-	1	1	1	
Rice	7	17	14	20	20	21	✓✓
Pasta and noodles	-	-	-	1	1	1	
Pizza	0	8	14	18	19	20	✓
Crisps and other savoury snacks	1	1	1	1	1	1	✓
Total Miscellaneous	-	-	-	3	4	4	-
Soups	-	-	-	0	0	0	x
Sauces and mayonnaise	2	3	4	1	1	1	✓
Ice cream and ice cream products	-	-	-	2	2	2	
Confectionery	-	-	-	0	0	0	x

(a) Percentage changes have not been included in this table due to the low reliability of the estimates
(b) Relative standard error. 3 ticks <2.5%, 2 ticks <5%, 1 tick < 10%, no ticks <20%, 1 cross >20%, - not available
 - Not available

Chapter 4 Trends in Household Expenditure

Headlines

In 2004-05 average UK expenditure on:

- all food and drink brought home was £23.05 per person per week, 1.4% lower in real terms
- food and non-alcoholic drinks brought home was £20.39 per person per week
- alcoholic drinks brought home was £2.66 per person per week

1. This section presents trends in household expenditure on food and drink that are brought into the home in the United Kingdom. Purchases may differ from actual food and drink consumption for a number of reasons e.g. food may be discarded during food preparation (e.g. vegetable peelings), food may be left on the plate at the end of a meal or food may become inedible before it can be consumed and is therefore thrown away. Purchases are recorded in the form in which they are bought. For example purchases of flour, fat, eggs and sugar are recorded as such, even if they are later used to bake a cake. If a ready-made cake is bought then it is recorded as cake.

2. Throughout the chapter figures used prior to 2001-02 are adjusted National Food Survey estimates. The adjustments brought the results of the National Food Survey into line with the Expenditure and Food Survey, and tended to increase estimates of expenditure on food and drink. The largest adjustments were for confectionery, alcoholic drinks, beverages and sugar and preserves. Adjustments for eggs and carcase meat resulted in reduced National Food Survey estimates. Details of the adjustments to the National Food Survey estimates can be found in Family Food 2002-03

3. More detailed series for 1974 to 2004-05 can be found on the Defra website. The most appropriate dataset to use for trends in UK household expenditure is: http://statistics.defra.gov.uk/esg/publications/efs/datasets/efsexpd.xls

Expenditure from 1974 to 2004-05 at current prices

4. Table 4.1 shows the trend in UK expenditure on food and drink at current prices. Trends shown at current prices reflect changes due to inflation as well as actual changes in expenditure.

5. Eating out data are only available from 1994 onwards. Data for food and drink eaten out are based on the National Food Survey and are considered less reliable than data based on the Expenditure and Food Survey (2001-02 onwards). This is especially true for data on alcohol consumed outside the home.

6. In 2004-05 average UK expenditure on food and drink (including alcoholic drinks) was £34.31 per person per week. Compared with the previous year expenditure on alcoholic drink in 2004-05 fell by 0.8 per cent and expenditure on other food and drink rose by 2.8 per cent.

Table 4.1 Trends in UK expenditure on food and drink at current prices

	1975(a)(c)	1985(a)(c)	1995(b)	2000(b)	2001-02	2002-03	2003-04	2004-05
								£ per person per week
Household food and drink			18.44	20.83	21.52	21.91	22.67	23.05
Food and drink eaten out			5.83(d)	7.36(d)	10.68	10.94	10.93	11.26
All food and drink			24.27	28.19	32.21	32.85	33.60	34.31
Household food and drink exc. alcohol	4.03	9.91	16.64	18.44	19.08	19.42	20.02	20.39
Food and drink eaten out exc. alcohol			4.31(d)	5.70(d)	6.98	7.21	7.33	7.72
All food and drink exc. alcohol			20.95	24.14	26.06	26.63	27.35	28.11
% eaten out			21%	24%	27%	27%	27%	27%
Household alcoholic drink			1.80	2.39	2.44	2.49	2.65	2.66
Eaten out alcoholic drink			1.52(d)	1.66(d)	3.71	3.73	3.60	3.54
All alcoholic drink			3.32	4.05	6.15	6.21	6.25	6.20
% eaten out			46%	41%	60%	60%	58%	57%

(a) Great Britain only
(b) Estimates of eating out in 1995 and 2000 are based on National Food Survey which was considered less reliable
(c) Excludes confectionery, soft and alcoholic drinks
(d) Whilst National Food Survey food household purchases were adjusted, eating out figures were not

Expenditure from 1974 to 2004-05 in real terms

7 Table 4.2 shows expenditure on food and drink in real terms from 1975 to 2004-05. The figures have been derived by deflating expenditure in current prices by the Retail Price Index. The figures do not represent a volume index for which the expenditure figures would have to be deflated using a price index for food only.

8 Figures for expenditure on all food and drink are not available for 1975 and 1985 because information on eating out was not collected in the National Food Survey before 1994.

Table 4.2 Trends in UK expenditure on food and drink in real terms at 2004-05 prices

	1975(a)(c)	1985(a)(c)	1995(a)(c)	2001-02	2002-03	2003-04	2004-05
							£ per person per week
Retail price index (1975 = 100)	100	277	436	508	519	534	550
Household food and drink			23.26	23.29	23.22	23.38	23.05
Food and drink eaten out			7.36(d)	11.56(d)	11.59	11.27	11.26
All food and drink			30.62	34.85	34.81	34.65	34.31
Household food and drink exc. alcohol	20.94	18.59	21.00	20.65	20.58	20.64	20.39
Food and drink eaten out exc. alcohol			5.44(d)	7.55(d)	7.64	7.55	7.72
All food and drink exc. alcohol			26.44	28.20	28.23	28.20	28.11
% eaten out			21%	27%	27%	27%	27%
Household alcoholic drink			2.27	2.64	2.64	2.73	2.66
Eaten out alcoholic drink			1.92(d)	4.01(d)	3.95	3.72	3.54
All alcholic drink			4.18	6.65	6.59	6.45	6.20
% eaten out			46%	60%	60%	58%	57%

(a) Great Britain only
(b) Estimates of eating out in 1995 and 2000 are based on National Food Survey which was considered less reliable
(c) Excludes confectionery, soft and alcoholic drinks
(d) Whilst National Food Survey household food purchases were adjusted, eating out figures were not

9 Between 1995 and 2004-05 expenditure on all food and drink increased by 12 per cent. Household expenditure fell by 0.9 per cent in real terms from 1995 whereas expenditure on food and drink eaten out rose by 53 per cent from £7.36 to £11.26 per person per week at 2004-05 prices.

10 Expenditure on food and drink excluding alcohol rose by 6.3 per cent in real terms between 1995 and 2004-05. Household expenditure fell by 2.9 per cent over the period, whereas eating out expenditure rose by 42 per cent.

11 Expenditure on alcoholic drinks rose by 48 per cent in real terms between 1995 and 2004-05. Expenditure on alcoholic drinks brought home rose by 17 per cent in real terms over the same period. Figures for expenditure on alcoholic drinks consumed outside the home prior to 2001-02 should be treated with caution because the results of the National Food Survey are thought to have under-recorded expenditure more than the Expenditure and Food Survey does. Expenditure on alcoholic drinks consumed outside the home has fallen slightly each year from 2001-02 to 2004-05.

12 The proportion of total expenditure, excluding that on alcoholic drinks, spent on eating out has been 27 per cent each year from 2001-02 to 2004-05. For alcoholic drinks expenditure is higher on drinks consumed outside the home than on drinks that are brought home. The proportion of expenditure spent on alcoholic drinks outside the home has fallen slightly each year from just over 60 per cent in 2001-02 to 57 per cent in 2004-05.

Prices

13 Food prices have tended to lag behind the Retail Price Index and fruit and vegetable prices have tended to lag behind the overall food price index. In 2001-02 there was an unusual rise in the price of fruit and vegetables which may explain the drop in consumption that year. In 2002-03 and 2003-04 fruit prices remained fairly stable but fell slightly in 2004-05. Vegetable prices fell back in 2002-03, rose in 2003-04 and fell slightly in 2004-05.

Table 4.3 Prices changes (1975=100)

	Retail price index	Food price index	Fruit price index	Vegetable price index
1975	100	100	100	100
1985	277	253	236	245
1995	436	364	291	303
2000	498	381	310	280
2001-02	508	397	342	325
2002-03	519	396	339	309
2003-04	534	404	346	335
2004-05	550	405	332	326

Chart 4.3 Prices changes since 1975 (1975=100)

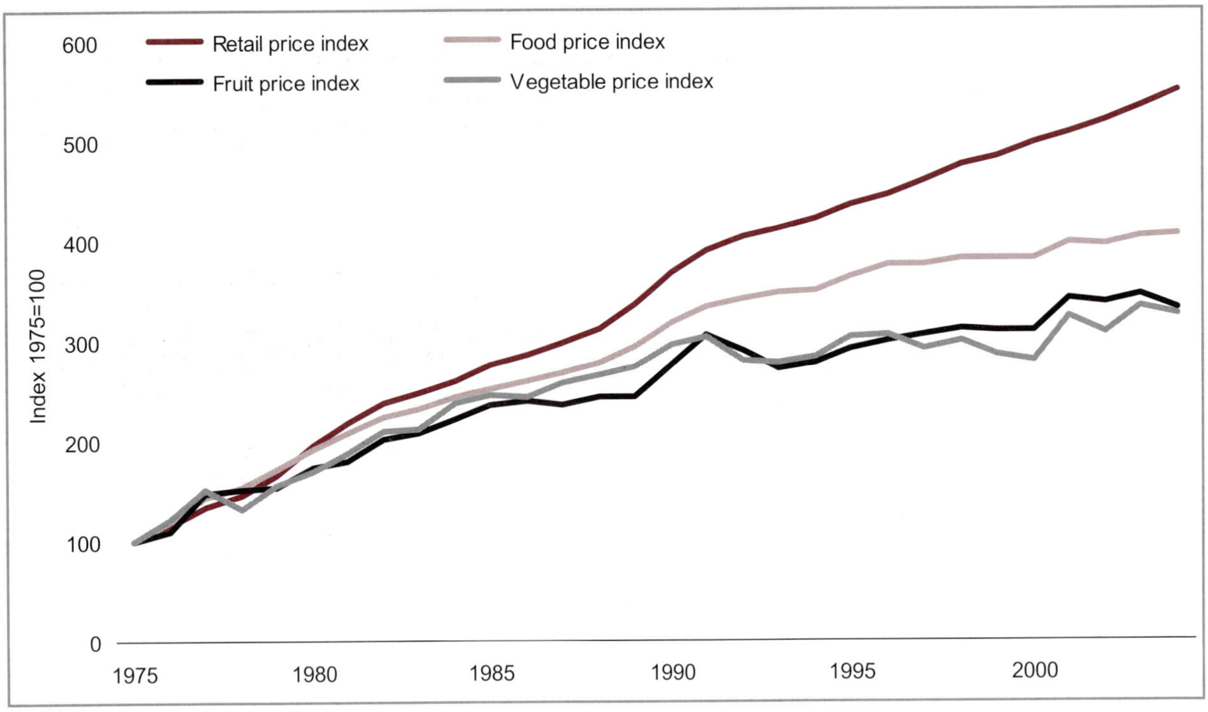

Milk, cream and cheese

14 Average expenditure on household purchases of milk and cream in 2004-05 was 156 pence per person per week, 1.7 per cent higher than in 2003-04 (see table 4.4). Average expenditure on cheese was 60 pence per person per week.

Table 4.4 UK household expenditure on milk, cream and cheese at current prices

	1974	1994	1999	2003-04	2004-05	Reliability of 2004-05 estimate (a)	% change since 2003-04
						pence per person per week	
Total milk and cream	29	150	141	154	156	✓✓✓	+ 1.7
Liquid wholemilk, full price	24	45	31	31	26	✓✓	- 17.8
Skimmed milks:	0	57	56	55	60	✓✓✓	+ 8.5
Fully skimmed	0	11	8	8	8	✓✓	+ 5.6
Semi and other skimmed	0	46	48	48	52	✓✓✓	+ 8.9
Other milks and dairy desserts (b)	2	15	18	25	25	-	+ 0.2
Yoghurt and fromage frais	1	27	30	36	40	✓✓✓	+ 10.0
Cream	2	5	6	5	5	✓✓	- 3.5
Total cheese	9	47	52	59	60	✓✓✓	+ 2.6
Natural cheese	8	42	47	51	53	✓✓✓	+ 3.6
Processed cheese	1	5	5	8	7	✓✓	- 3.8

(a) Relative standard error. 3 ticks <2.5%, 2 ticks <5%, 1 tick < 10%, no ticks <20%, 1 cross >20%, - not available
(b) Includes condensed, infant and instant milks

Meat, fish and eggs

15 Average expenditure on household purchases of meat, fish and eggs in 2004-05 was £6.11 per person per week, a rise of 1.0 per cent on the previous year (see table 4.5). Of this, £3.80 per person per week was spent on meat products, £1.14 on carcase meat, 99 pence on fish and 18 pence on eggs.

Table 4.5 UK household expenditure on meat, fish and eggs at current prices

	1974	1994	1999	2003-04	2004-05	Reliability of 2004-05 estimate (a)	% change since 2003-04
						\multicolumn{2}{r}{pence per person per week}
Total meat and meat products	100	390	425	493	494	✓✓✓	+ 0.2
Carcase	44	105	98	111	114	✓✓✓	+ 2.9
Beef and veal	24	56	49	60	64	✓✓✓	+ 6.0
Mutton and lamb	11	23	25	27	25	✓✓	- 4.2
Pork	9	26	24	24	24	✓✓	+ 2.8
Non-carcase	56	285	327	382	380	✓✓✓	- 0.6
Bacon and ham, uncooked	13	30	32	37	37	✓✓✓	+ 0.1
Bacon and ham, cooked (b)	4	21	24	35	33	✓✓✓	- 4.7
Poultry, uncooked	8	47	56	69	69	-	+ 0.1
Poultry, cooked (b)	1	10	21	25	26	✓✓	+ 4.5
Ready meals	2	48	57	70	69	✓✓✓	- 2.1
Other	27	130	137	146	146	-	- 0.2
Total fish	14	73	83	94	99	✓✓✓	+ 5.4
White, fresh chilled and frozen	5	19	19	17	16	✓✓	- 1.8
Herrings and other blue fish, fresh chilled and frozen	0	1	3	4	4	✓	- 8.2
Salmon, fresh chilled and frozen	0	2	6	7	8	✓	+ 6.1
Blue fish, dried salted and smoked	0	3	3	4	5	✓	+ 20.6
White fish, dried salted and smoked	1	3	4	3	3	✓	+ 15.4
Shellfish	0	5	5	9	10	✓	+ 4.4
Takeaway fish	2	13	10	12	14	✓✓	+ 9.2
Salmon, canned	1	4	3	3	3	✓	- 0.7
Other canned or bottled fish	1	6	8	9	10	✓✓	+ 6.7
Ready meals	2	15	11	21	23	✓✓	+ 7.8
Takeaway fish meals	0	3	11	4	4	✓	+ 5.0
Eggs	11	16	16	18	18	✓✓✓	+ 1.8

(a) Relative standard error. 3 ticks <2.5%, 2 ticks <5%, 1 tick < 10%, no ticks <20%, 1 cross >20%, - not available
(b) Excludes canned

Fats

16 In 2004-05 about 37 pence per person per week was spent on fats and oils (see table 4.6). This was 3.8 per cent more than in 2003-04.

Table 4.6 UK household expenditure on fats and oils at current prices

	1974	1994	1999	2003-04	2004-05	Reliability of 2004-05 estimate (a)	% change since 2003-04
						pence per person per week	
Total fats and oils	15	37	36	36	37	✓✓✓	+ 3.8
Butter	7	9	10	10	11	✓✓	+ 5.1
Margarine	3	5	2	1	1	✓	- 12.2
Low fat and reduced fat spreads	0	14	14	14	14	-	+ 0.5
Reduced fat spreads	0	9	10	11	8	✓✓	- 25.2
Low fat spreads	0	4	4	3	6	✓✓	+ 99.9
Vegetable and salad oils	1	5	6	7	8	✓✓	+ 9.9
Other fats and oils (including lard)	3	4	3	3	3	-	+ 8.3

(a) Relative standard error. 3 ticks <2.5%, 2 ticks <5%, 1 tick < 10%, no ticks <20%, 1 cross >20%, - not available

Sugar and preserves

17 In 2004-05 about 17 pence per person was spent each week on household purchases of sugar and preserves (see table 4.7).

Table 4.7 UK household expenditure on sugar and preserves at current prices

	1974	1994	1999	2003-04	2004-05	Reliability of 2004-05 estimate (a)	% change since 2003-04
						pence per person per week	
Total sugar and preserves	9	20	17	16	17	✓✓✓	+ 6.7
Sugar	6	12	9	8	8	✓✓	+ 3.7
Honey, preserves, syrup and treacle	3	8	8	8	9	✓✓	+ 9.5

Fruit and vegetables

18 In 2004-05 just over £1.00 was spent per person per week on household purchases of fresh and processed potatoes, £1.82 was spent on vegetables excluding potatoes and £1.67 was spent on fruit (see table 4.8).

Table 4.8 UK household expenditure on fruit and vegetables at current prices

	1974	1994	1999	2003-04	2004-05	Reliability of 2004-05 estimate (a)	% change since 2004-05
						pence per person per week	
Total vegetables including potatoes	41	225	274	279	284	✓✓✓	+ 1.6
Fresh potatoes	8	29	34	32	34	✓✓✓	+ 4.9
Processed potatoes	6	63	79	70	68	✓✓✓	- 2.9
Total vegetables excluding potatoes	27	133	162	177	182	✓✓✓	+ 2.8
Fresh green vegetables	6	25	34	43	43	✓✓✓	- 0.2
Fresh cabbages	2	4	4	4	4	✓✓	+ 3.5
Fresh cauliflowers	1	8	8	9	9	✓✓✓	+ 1.7
Other fresh vegetables	10	52	65	80	85	✓✓✓	+ 5.3
Fresh carrots	1	6	6	6	7	✓✓✓	+ 14.9
Onions, leeks and shallots	1	8	9	11	11	✓✓✓	+ 2.2
Fresh tomatoes	4	12	15	19	19	✓✓✓	- 0.4
Miscellaneous other fresh vegetables	1	10	16	23	26	✓✓✓	+ 10.8
All frozen vegetables (b)	3	16	16	10	9	✓✓	- 14.6
Other vegetables, not frozen (c)	8	40	46	44	46	-	+ 5.2
Total fruit	21	112	143	163	167	✓✓✓	+ 2.7
Fresh fruit	12	74	95	115	119	✓✓✓	+ 3.2
Fresh apples	4	18	19	22	21	✓✓✓	- 2.4
Fresh bananas	2	16	22	19	19	✓✓✓	- 2.7
Fruit juices	1	18	27	25	23	✓✓✓	- 10.5
Other fruit products	8	20	20	22	26	-	+ 15.1

(a) Relative standard error. 3 ticks <2.5%, 2 ticks <5%, 1 tick < 10%, no ticks <20%, 1 cross >20%, - not available
(b) Excludes potato products
(c) Mainly processed tomatoes, peas and beans and ready meals

Bread, cereals and cereal products

19 In 2004-05 an average of £3.76 was spent per person per week on household purchases of bread, cereals and cereal products (see table 4.9). Of this, 93 pence was spent on bread and £1.06 on cakes, pastries and biscuits.

Table 4.9 UK household expenditure on bread, cereals and cereal products at current prices

	1974	1994	1999	2003-04	2004-05	Reliability of 2004-05 estimate (a)	% change since 2004-05
						pence per person per week	
Total cereals including bread	58	271	323	368	376	✓✓✓	+ 2.1
Bread	21	75	80	90	93	✓✓✓	+ 3.4
White bread	16	29	30	33	31	✓✓✓	- 6.6
Brown bread	2	8	7	4	4	✓✓✓	+ 23.3
Wholemeal bread	0	9	8	9	12	✓✓✓	+ 24.2
Rolls and sandwiches	2	18	19	22	23	-	+ 6.0
Other bread	1	11	15	21	22	-	+ 3.9
Cereals excluding bread	37	196	244	278	283	✓✓	+ 1.7
Flour	2	3	2	2	3	✓✓✓	+ 13.0
Cakes and pastries	11	49	53	52	52	-	+ 0.6
Buns, scones and tea-cakes	2	9	10	10	12	✓✓✓	+ 14.5
Biscuits	12	45	49	51	54	✓✓✓	+ 4.2
Oatmeal and oat products	0	1	2	2	2	✓✓✓	+ 16.7
Breakfast cereals	4	32	34	37	37	✓✓✓	0.0
Rice	1	6	16	22	23	✓✓✓	+ 3.0
Pasta	1	3	11	14	14	✓✓✓	+ 1.4
Pizza	0	19	35	43	43	✓✓✓	+ 0.1
Other cereals	5	30	33	45	44	-	- 1.5

(a) Relative standard error. 3 ticks <2.5%, 2 ticks <5%, 1 tick < 10%, no ticks <20%, 1 cross >20%, - not available

Beverages and miscellaneous foods

20 In 2004-05 42 pence per person per week was spent on household purchases of beverages, mainly tea and coffee (see table 4.10).

Table 4.10 UK expenditure on beverages and miscellaneous food and drink at current prices

	1974	1994	1999	2003-04	2004-05	Reliability of 2004-05 estimate (a)	% change since 2003-04
						pence per person per week	
Total beverages	12	50	49	41	42	✓✓✓	+ 1.1
Tea	6	20	19	16	16	✓✓✓	0.0
Coffee	5	23	22	21	21	-	+ 1.1
Cocoa and drinking chocolate	1	2	4	2	2	✓	- 1.4
Branded food drinks	1	5	4	2	2	✓	+ 7.4
Total miscellaneous	12	78	96	118	123	✓✓✓	+ 4.3
Mineral water	0	5	8	9	10	✓✓	+ 10.5
Soups	3	10	12	13	14	-	+ 9.0
Pickles and sauces	2	19	28	32	33	✓✓✓	+ 2.9
Ice-cream and ice-cream products	2	17	19	22	21	✓✓	- 4.8
Other foods (b)	6	26	31	40	45	-	+ 11.8

(a) Relative standard error. 3 ticks <2.5%, 2 ticks <5%, 1 tick < 10%, no ticks <20%, 1 cross >20%, - not available
(b) Includes spreads, dressings, salt and other miscellaneous food items

Soft and alcoholic drinks and confectionery

21 In 2004-05 about 80 pence per person per week was spent on household purchases of soft drinks (excluding fruit juices) (see table 4.11). About four times that amount was spent on alcoholic drinks when expenditure per person was adjusted to exclude people under 14 years of age. Sales of wine rose again, continuing the trend over the last ten years. Over the same period sales of traditional beers were static, while lagers and continental beers showed a steady upward trend, though not as pronounced as that for wine.

Table 4.11 UK household expenditure on soft and alcoholic drinks and confectionary at current prices

	1994	1999	2003-04	2004-05	Reliability of 2004-05 estimate (a)	% change since 2003-04
						pence per person per week
Total soft drinks (b) (c)	48	61	83	80	✓✓✓	- 3.5
Concentrated (c)	11	11	11	11	✓✓	- 4.6
Ready to drink	23	31	50	50	✓✓✓	0.0
Low-calorie, concentrated (c)	4	4	2	2	✓	- 5.7
Low-calorie, ready to drink	11	15	19	17	✓✓	- 11.6
Total alcoholic drinks (average for whole population)	152	208	265	266	✓✓✓	+ 0.4
Beer (d)	19	21	19	18	✓	- 5.6
Lager and continental beer (d)	26	36	51	49	✓✓	- 5.6
Wine	55	90	118	131	✓✓	+ 10.5
Other (e)	53	62	76	68	-	- 10.0
Estimated average alcoholic drink purchases by people aged 14 or over						
Total	-	-	321	321	-	+ 0.2
Beer (d)	-	-	24	22	-	- 5.7
Lager and continental beer (d)	-	-	62	59	-	- 5.7
Wine	-	-	143	158	-	+ 10.3
Other (e)	-	-	92	82	-	- 10.1
Total confectionery	60	67	81	84	✓✓✓	+ 3.9
Solid chocolate	13	15	18	20	✓✓	+ 12.3
Chocolate coated bars/sweets	30	34	39	40	✓✓	+ 2.9
Mints and boiled sweets	13	14	19	18	✓✓	- 2.7
Other	3	4	5	6	-	+ 5.9

(a) Relative standard error. 3 ticks <2.5%, 2 ticks <5%, 1 tick < 10%, no ticks <20%, 1 cross >20%, - not available
(b) Excluding pure fruit juices which are recorded in the survey under fruit products
(c) Converted to unconcentrated equivalent
(d) Including low alcohol lager and beers
(e) Including ciders, perrys, fortified wines, spirits, liqueurs and alcoholic carbonates
- Not available

Takeaway foods brought home

22 There was no significant change in household expenditure on takeaway food purchases in 2004-05 compared with the previous year (see table 4.12).

Table 4.12 UK household expenditure on takeaway food at current prices

	1974	1994	1999	2002-03	2003-04	2004-05	Reliability of 2004-05 estimate (b)
						pence per person per week	
Total Meat	1	56	75	63	66	67	-
Chicken	0	1	7	5	5	6	✓
Meat pies and pasties	0	3	4	2	2	2	✓
Burger and bun	0	6	7	5	6	6	✓
Kebabs	0	6	7	6	7	7	✓
Sausages and saveloys	0	1	1	2	2	2	✓
Meat Based meals	1	40	48	41	45	44	✓✓
Miscellaneous meats	0	0	1	0	0	0	x
Total Fish	3	15	21	17	17	18	-
Fish	2	13	10	13	12	14	✓✓
Fish products	0	1	1	1	1	1	
Fish based meals	0	2	10	4	4	4	✓
Total Vegetables	2	19	25	25	26	27	-
Chips	2	15	16	19	18	19	✓✓
Vegetable takeaway products	0	4	9	6	7	8	✓
Total Bread	-	-	-	5	6	6	-
Sandwiches	0	1	2	2	3	3	✓
Breads	-	-	-	3	3	3	✓
Total Other cereals	-	-	-	36	38	38	-
Pastries	-	-	-	1	1	1	
Rice	0	2	7	12	13	13	✓✓
Pasta and noodles	-	-	-	1	1	1	
Pizza	0	5	14	20	22	22	✓
Crisps and other savoury snacks	0	1	1	1	2	2	✓
Total Miscellaneous	-	-	-	3	3	3	-
Soups	-	-	-	0	0	0	x
Sauces and mayonnaise	0	1	1	1	1	1	✓
Ice cream and ice cream products	-	-	-	1	1	1	
Confectionery	-	-	-	0	0	0	x

(a) Percentage changes have not been included in this table due to the low reliability of the estimates
(b) Relative standard error. 3 ticks <2.5%, 2 ticks <5%, 1 tick < 10%, no ticks <20%, 1 cross >20%, - not available
 - Not available

Chapter 5 Trends in Household Nutrient Intakes

Headlines

In 2004-05, estimated average intakes of

- energy from household purchases of food and drink (excluding alcohol) fell by 1.3 per cent when compared with 2003-04 and fell by 4.9 per cent when compared with 1994
- fibre from household purchases had risen slightly since 1994
- sodium from household purchases fell by 1.4 per cent compared with 2003-04 and fell by 2.5 per cent when compared with 1994
- intakes of iron, zinc, magnesium and potassium were below recommended levels

In 2004-05, as a percentage of food and drink energy excluding alcohol, estimated average intakes of

- saturated fatty acids from household purchases decreased by 0.7 per cent compared with 2003-04 and decreased by 2.9 per cent compared with 1994
- poly-unsaturated fatty acids from household purchases decreased by 0.1 per cent compared with 2003-04 and decreased by 0.4 per cent compared with 1994
- carbohydrate from household purchases were the same as 2003-04 and fell by 0.2 per cent compared with 1994
- non-milk extrinsic sugars from household purchases fell by 0.5 per cent compared with 2003-04 and fell by 3.0 per cent compared with 1994
- protein from household purchases increased by 0.8 per cent compared with 2003-04 and increased by 10 per cent compared with 1994

[1] This chapter looks at the energy and nutrient intakes derived from household purchases of food and drink from 1994. The figures are based on adjusted National Food Survey results up to 2000 and Expenditure and Food Survey results from 2001-02 onwards. For more detail on how the adjustments to the National Food Survey results were carried out see Family Food in 2002-03.

[2] More detailed series for all years from 1974 onwards can be found on the Defra website along with estimates for some types of food and some nutritional intakes going back to 1940. These series, in particular those for energy, non-milk extrinsic sugars, fat and alcohol, are affected by the inclusion since 1992 of the contributions from alcoholic drinks, confectionery and soft drinks brought into the household. Because of these breaks in the series this chapter concentrates on trends that have emerged over the last ten years.

[3] Table 5.1 shows energy and nutrient intakes from household food and drink since 1994. It also shows average intakes of fat, fatty acids, carbohydrate and protein as percentages of energy

excluding alcohol intake and average energy and nutrient intakes as percentages of weighted reference nutrient intake[1].

Table 5.1 Trends in UK estimated intakes from household food and drink 1994 to 2004-05

		1994	1999	2003-04	2004-05	% change since 2003-04
						intake per person per day
Energy	kcal	2 137	2 056	2 077	2 048	- 1.4
	MJ	9.0	8.6	8.7	8.6	- 1.4
Energy excluding alcohol	kcal	2 101	2 012	2 025	1 998	- 1.3
Total Protein	g	67.5	68.5	71.0	70.6	- 0.5
Animal Protein	g	40.9	40.6	43.6	43.1	- 1.1
Fat	g	91	83	85	83	- 1.7
Fatty acids:						
Saturates	g	35.7	32.8	33.6	32.9	- 2.0
Mono-unsaturates	g	33.5	29.5	30.6	30.2	- 1.5
Poly-unsaturates	g	15.4	14.5	14.8	14.6	- 1.4
Cholesterol	mg	243	228	237	230	- 2.7
Carbohydrate (b)	g	270	265	261	257	- 1.3
Total sugars	g	129	123	124	123	- 1.4
Non-milk extrinsic sugars	g	87	82	82	80	- 1.8
Starch	g	141	141	136	134	- 1.3
Fibre (c)	g	13	13	13	13	+ 0.6
Alcohol	g	5.1	6.3	7.4	7.2	- 2.6
Calcium	mg	899	881	927	904	- 2.5
Iron	mg	11.0	10.9	11.2	11.2	- 0.6
Zinc	mg	8.4	8.0	8.4	8.3	- 0.1
Magnesium	mg	256	255	254	256	+ 0.7
Sodium (d)	g	2.78	2.79	2.75	2.71	- 1.4
Potassium	g	2.81	2.86	2.86	2.86	+ 0.1
Thiamin	mg	1.38	1.44	1.56	1.56	0.0
Riboflavin	mg	1.74	1.82	1.85	1.80	- 2.7
Niacin equivalent	mg	27.2	28.3	30.8	30.7	- 0.1
Vitamin B6	mg	2.0	2.1	2.2	2.2	- 1.0
Vitamin B12	µg	5.3	7.4	6.1	5.9	- 4.0
Folate	µg	257	254	258	257	- 0.2
Vitamin C	mg	65	67	67	64	- 4.7
Vitamin A:						
Retinol	µg	1 016	596	513	470	- 8.5
β-carotene	µg	1 863	1 889	1 801	1 832	+ 1.7
Retinol equivalent	µg	1 327	911	817	782	- 4.3
Vitamin D	µg	2.78	3.26	2.92	2.89	- 1.1
Vitamin E	mg	10.82	11.06	11.15	10.66	- 4.4
		as a percentage of food and drink energy excluding alcohol				
Fat	%	38.8	37.0	37.7	37.6	- 0.3
Fatty acids:						
Saturates	%	15.3	14.7	14.9	14.8	- 0.7
Mono-unsaturates	%	14.3	13.2	13.6	13.6	- 0.1
Poly-unsaturates	%	6.6	6.5	6.6	6.6	- 0.1
Carbohydrate	%	48.2	49.3	48.3	48.3	0.0
Non-milk extrinsic sugars	%	15.5	15.2	15.1	15.0	- 0.5
Protein	%	12.8	13.6	14.0	14.1	+ 0.8

continued

---

[1] Department of Health, *'Dietary Reference Values for Food Energy and Nutrients for the United Kingdom'*, HMSO 1991

Table 5.1 continued

		1994	1999	2003-04	2004-05	% change since 2003-04
		\multicolumn{5}{r}{as a percentage of weighted reference nutrient intake (e)}
Energy (f)	%	93	89	89	88	- 1.3
Energy excluding alcohol (f)	%	91	87	87	86	- 1.3
Protein	%	136	137	140	139	- 0.5
Calcium	%	119	116	121	118	- 2.5
Iron	%	96	95	98	97	- 0.5
Zinc	%	96	92	94	94	- 0.1
Magnesium	%	88	88	86	87	+ 0.7
Sodium (d)	%	170	170	165	163	- 1.4
Potassium	%	81	82	81	81	+ 0.1
Thiamin	%	149	155	167	167	0.0
Riboflavin	%	139	145	146	142	- 2.7
Niacin equivalent	%	178	185	199	199	- 0.1
Vitamin B6	%	148	157	161	159	- 1.0
Vitamin B12	%	353	484	397	381	- 4.0
Folate	%	125	123	123	123	- 0.1
Vitamin C	%	154	158	157	150	- 4.7
Vitamin A (retinol equivalent)	%	194	133	118	113	- 4.3

(a) Contributions from pharmaceutical sources are not recorded by the survey
(b) Available carbohydrate, calculated as monosaccharide equivalent
(c) As non-starch polysaccharides
(d) (i) Excludes sodium from table salt (ii) The RNI for sodium is the amount that is sufficient for 97 per cent of the population. In May 2003 the Scientific Advisory Committee on Nutrition made recommendations about the maximum amount of salt that people should be eating, i.e. that the average salt intake for adults should be no more than 6 grams per day, equivalent to 2.4 grams of sodium per day
(e) Department of Health, 'Dietary Reference Values for Food Energy and Nutrients for the United Kingdom', HMSO 1991
(f) As a percentage of Estimated Average Requirement

Energy

4 Average energy intake from household food and drink (excluding alcohol) showed a gradual decline from 2101 kcal in 1994 to 1998 kcal per person per day in 2004-05. There was a 1.3 per cent decrease in 2004-05 compared with 2003-04 (see also chart 2.2).

Protein, fat and cholesterol

5 Average intake of protein from household food remained fairly stable at 70.6 grams per person per day in 2004-05.

6 Compared with 2003-04 there was a small decrease in the average intake of fat in 2004-05 to 83 grams per person per day, reflecting the drop in energy intake. Since 1994 there has been little change in the proportions of saturated, mono-unsaturated fatty acids and poly-unsaturated fatty acids that make up the total intake of fatty acids. The percentage of food energy intake derived from fat has fallen only slightly from 39 per cent in 1994 to 38 per cent in 2004-05 and remains above the 35 per cent recommended by COMA in 1991 (see also the "Fat intake and saturated fatty acid intake" section of Chapter 2). The percentage of food energy intake derived from saturated fatty acids was 15 per cent in 2004-05 which is also higher than the 11 per cent recommendation made by COMA in 1991.

7 The average intake of cholesterol fell by 2.7 per cent in 2004-05 compared with the previous year to 230 milligrams per person per day.

Carbohydrate, non-milk extrinsic sugars and starch

8. The decline in the average intake of carbohydrate from household food and drink which began in 2000 continued with a year-on-year decrease of 1.3 per cent in 2004-05 to 257 grams per person per day, in line with the fall in energy intake. Since 1994 there has been an overall 4.7 per cent fall in the average intake of carbohydrate, but there has been little change in the percentage of food energy intake derived from carbohydrate.

9. The average intake of non-milk extrinsic sugars (principally added sugars) from household food and drink fell by 1.3 per cent compared with 2003-04 to 80 grams per person per day in 2004-05. This was 15 per cent of food energy intake in 2004-05 which is above the 11 per cent recommendation made by COMA in 1991. There was also a 1.3 per cent fall in the average intake of starch of to 134 grams per person per day.

Fibre

10. In 2004-05 there was a slight increase in the average intake of fibre to 13.2 grams per person per day (expressed as non-starch polysaccharides) from household food, but there is no trend.

Alcohol

11. The average intake of alcohol from household food and drink decreased by 2.6 per cent in 2004-05 to 7.2 grams per person per day compared with 7.4 grams the previous year.

Minerals

12. The average intake of calcium fell by 2.5 per cent in 2004-05 compared with 2003-04, to 904 milligrams per person per day due to the decrease in purchases of milk, milk products and bread. There was little change in the average intakes of iron, zinc, magnesium and potassium for 2004-05 compared with 2003-04. All four were below recommended levels.

13. The average intake of sodium (excluding sodium from table salt) started to fall in 2001-02 and this trend continued in 2004-05 with a year-on-year decrease of 1.4 per cent to an average intake of 2.71 grams of sodium per person per day.

Vitamins

14. Vitamin intakes from household food continued to show few clear long-term trends. The 4.7 per cent decrease in the average intake of vitamin C from 67 milligrams per person per day in 2003-04 to 64 milligrams per person per day in 2004-05 was mainly due to the reduction in purchases of processed fruit.

15. The average intake of vitamin A (retinol equivalent) decreased by 4.3 per cent from 817 micrograms per person per day in 2003-04 to 782 micrograms in 2004-05 as the result of the reduction in purchases of non-carcase meat and meat products.

16 The 4.4 per cent decrease in vitamin E was largely due to revisions to the nutrient composition data for spreads based on newly available manufacturers' data.

Contributions by household food types to intakes

17 Table 5.2 shows how different types of household food and drink purchases contributed to estimated intakes of selected macronutrients and micronutrients in 2004-05.

18 The major sources of energy were bread and other cereal products, and non-carcase meat and meat products.

- Fat was obtained mainly from purchases of fats and oils such as butter and other spreads, but also from meat and meat products and milk and milk products.

- Calcium came mainly from milk, milk products and bread, and iron mainly from bread and other cereal products.

- Non-milk extrinsic sugars came mainly from purchases of sugar and preserves, soft drinks and confectionery.

- Sodium (excluding that from table salt) came mainly from other meat and meat products, bread, and food in the "other food" category (mainly sauces).

- Vitamin C came mainly from processed and fresh fruit (including fruit juice), whilst β-carotene came mainly from vegetables.

- Vitamin A intake came mainly from non-carcass meat and meat products, milk and dairy products and vegetables.

Table 5.2 Estimated intakes from different types of household food

	Energy	Fat	Saturated fatty acids	Calcium	Iron	Non-milk extrinsic sugars	Sodium	Folate	Vitamin C	β-carotene	Vitamin A (Retinol equiv.)
										average per person per day	
	kcal	grams	grams	mg	mg	grams	mg	µg	mg	µg	µg
Milk and cream (a)	175	7.7	4.8	347	0.2	2.8	134	19.2	3.9	42	91
Cheese	57	4.7	3.0	94	0.0	0.0	114	4.8	0.0	21	52
Carcase meat	63	4.2	1.8	2	0.4	0.0	20	3.2	0.0	0	1
Other meat and meat products	223	14.1	5.1	32	1.2	0.1	607	11.8	2.5	78	154
Fish	31	1.5	0.4	15	0.2	0.0	79	3.3	0.1	4	4
Eggs	17	1.3	0.4	6	0.2	0.0	16	5.7	0.0	0	22
Fats	172	18.8	5.7	4	0.0	0.2	103	0.0	0.0	87	154
Sugar and preserves	69	0.0	0.0	3	0.1	18.1	4	0.1	0.4	1	0
Fresh potatoes	49	0.1	0.0	3	0.3	0.0	5	22.0	4.0	0	0
Fresh green vegetables	6	0.1	0.0	9	0.2	0.0	2	16.5	2.8	79	13
Other fresh vegetables	16	0.2	0.0	14	0.3	0.0	9	17.0	5.3	997	166
Processed vegetables	131	5.6	1.8	25	0.9	1.0	246	20.2	6.3	253	46
Fresh fruit	48	0.4	0.1	12	0.2	0.0	3	8.7	16.1	33	5
Processed fruit	46	1.8	0.4	9	0.2	5.4	13	9.3	14.6	10	2
Bread	229	2.5	0.6	146	1.8	0.1	497	29.6	0.0	1	5
Flour	27	0.1	0.0	11	0.2	0.0	0	1.9	0.0	0	0
Cakes, buns and pastries	81	3.2	1.4	18	0.3	5.8	73	2.6	0.1	3	9
Biscuits	113	5.2	2.6	24	0.5	5.6	88	2.6	0.0	0	0
Other cereal products (b)	213	4.2	1.5	64	2.8	4.4	245	50.8	0.4	42	21
Beverages	6	0.1	0.0	6	0.2	0.7	7	9.8	0.0	0	2
Other food (c)	74	4.1	1.4	22	0.4	5.8	401	11.6	0.7	93	16
Soft drinks	66	0.0	0.0	10	0.0	17.4	18	2.3	6.9	80	13
Confectionery	82	3.4	1.9	20	0.2	11.4	18	1.5	0.0	6	5
Alcoholic drinks	56	0.0	0.0	7	0.3	1.2	7	2.6	0.0	0	0
Total household intake	**2 048**	**83**	**33**	**904**	**11**	**80**	**2 709**	**257**	**64**	**1 832**	**782**
	as a percentage of total intake per person per day from household purchases										
	%	%	%	%	%	%	%	%	%	%	%
Milk and cream (a)	9	9	15	38	2	4	5	7	6	2	12
Cheese	3	6	9	10	0	0	4	2	0	1	7
Carcase meat	3	5	5	0	4	0	1	1	0	0	0
Other meat and meat products	11	17	16	4	10	0	22	5	4	4	20
Fish	2	2	1	2	2	0	3	1	0	0	0
Eggs	1	2	1	1	2	0	1	2	0	0	3
Fats	8	22	17	0	0	0	4	0	0	5	20
Sugar and preserves	3	0	0	0	1	23	0	0	1	0	0
Fresh potatoes	2	0	0	0	2	0	0	9	6	0	0
Fresh green vegetables	0	0	0	1	2	0	0	6	4	4	2
Other fresh vegetables	1	0	0	2	3	0	0	7	8	54	21
Processed vegetables	6	7	6	3	8	1	9	8	10	14	6
Fresh fruit	2	0	0	1	2	0	0	3	25	2	1
Processed fruit	2	2	1	1	2	7	0	4	23	1	0
Bread	11	3	2	16	16	0	18	12	0	0	1
Flour	1	0	0	1	1	0	0	1	0	0	0
Cakes, buns and pastries	4	4	4	2	3	7	3	1	0	0	1
Biscuits	6	6	8	3	5	7	3	1	0	0	0
Other cereal products (b)	10	5	4	7	25	5	9	20	1	2	3
Beverages	0	0	0	1	2	1	0	4	0	0	0
Other food (c)	4	5	4	2	3	7	15	4	1	5	2
Soft drinks	3	0	0	1	0	22	1	1	11	4	2
Confectionery	4	4	6	2	2	14	1	1	0	0	1
Alcoholic drinks	3	0	0	1	3	1	0	1	0	0	0

(a) Includes all whole and skimmed liquid and instant milks, yoghurt and fromage frais, milk desserts and cream.
(b) Includes oatmeal and oat products, breakfast cereals, canned milk puddings, other puddings such as sponge puddings and pies, rice, cereal-based invalid foods, slimming foods, infant foods, frozen cakes and pastries, pasta, pizza, cereal convenience foods such as cake, pudding and dessert mixes, custard powder, other cereals such as barley, cous cous, corn and tapioca.
(c) Includes mineral or spring waters, baby foods, soups, other takeaway food brought home, meals on wheels, salad dressings and other spreads & dressings, pickles, sauces, takeaway sauces and mayonnnais, stock cubes and meat & yeast extracts, jelly squares or crystals, ice cream (all types), salt, artificial sweeteners, vinegar, spices and dried herbs, bisto, gravy granules, stuffing mix, baking powder, yeast, fruit, herbal and instant teas, and soya and novel protein foods.

Chapter 6 Food and Drink Purchased for Consumption Outside the Home

Headlines

In 2004-05, compared with 2003-04,

- there was a 6.7 per cent decrease in the average number of items of food or drink purchased per person per year for consumption outside the home

- average weekly expenditure on food and drink purchased for consumption outside the home rose by 3.0 per cent to £11.26 per person, broadly in-line with inflation

- estimated average intake of energy (excluding alcohol) from food and drink purchased for consumption outside the home decreased by 6.7 per cent

- people derived an average of 7.6 per cent of their energy intake (excluding alcohol) from food and drink purchased for consumption outside the home

- purchases of alcoholic drinks for consumption outside the home fell by 7.3 per cent (and were 16 per cent lower than in 2001-02)

- purchases of soft drinks for consumption outside the home fell by 8.9 per cent

- purchases of confectionery eaten out fell by 16 per cent

- purchases of crisps, nuts and snacks eaten out fell by 19 per cent

- purchases of Indian, Chinese and Thai meals or dishes eaten out rose by 6.7 per cent

- purchases of rice, pasta and noodles eaten out rose by 7.6 per cent

1. This section shows detailed information on food and drink purchased for consumption outside the home (i.e. 'eaten out') from the Expenditure and Food Survey from 2001-02 onwards. Whilst year on year changes can look quite large it should be remembered that 'eating out' purchases account for less than 10 per cent of total purchases of food and drink. Note that free food, such as free school meals, is not included in these results.

2. Further estimates are available from the National Food Survey from 1994 to 2000 but these are considered to be of lower quality due to problems with data collection. These data are still of value at aggregated levels and as an indication of trends over time. They have been used in table 6.4 to compile estimates of intakes of energy, fat and non-milk extrinsic sugars (mainly added sugars) from eating out.

Purchases of food and drink for consumption outside the home

3. Table 6.1 shows both the quantity of food and drink purchased for consumption outside the home and the total expenditure. The average quantity of alcoholic drinks purchased for consumption outside the home was an 616 millilitres per person per week in 2004-05. This represented a 7.3 per cent drop compared to the previous year. There was an associated 7.7 per cent drop in intake

of alcohol – see Table 6.3. As in previous years purchases of soft drinks were substantially lower than purchases of alcoholic drinks. The quantity of soft drinks purchased for consumption outside the home decreased by 8.9 per cent in 2004-05 to an average of 350 millilitres per person per week. Purchases of beverages (mainly tea and coffee) fell by 0.8 per cent from 142 millilitres in 2003-04 to 141 millilitres per person per week in 2004-05.

4 Purchases of meat and meat products eaten out fell by 6.0 per cent between 2003-04 and 2004-05, from 97 to 91 grams per person per week. Purchases of potatoes and potato products eaten out fell by 4.7 per cent over the same period, from 83 to 79 grams per person per week. Purchases of sandwiches eaten out fell by 7.5 per cent from 76 to 71 grams per person per week.

5 The largest increase in purchases between 2003-04 and 2004-05 was for rice, pasta and noodles, a rise of 7.6 per cent. Food purchases (i.e. excluding drinks) fell 19 per cent for crisps, nuts and snacks, 16 per cent for confectionery and 7.5 per cent for sandwiches.

6 Expenditure on food and non-alcoholic drinks purchased for consumption outside the home was 5.3 per cent higher in 2004-05 compared with 2003-04 at an average of £7.72 per person per week. Expenditure on alcoholic drinks purchased for consumption outside the home was 1.7 per cent lower in 2004-05, falling from an average of £3.60 to £3.54 per person per week.

Table 6.1 UK average purchases of food and drink for consumption outside the home

		2001-02	2002-03	2003-04	2004-05	Reliability of 2004-05 estimate (a)	% change since 2003-04
					grams per person per week unless otherwise stated		
Alcoholic drinks							
average across whole population	ml	732	702	664	616	✓✓	- 7.3
average excluding under 14's	ml	893	850	803	743	✓✓	- 7.4
Soft drinks inc. milk drinks	ml	373	376	384	350	✓✓✓	- 8.9
Beverages	ml	154	147	142	141	✓✓	- 0.8
Meat and meat products		94	95	97	91	✓✓✓	- 6.0
Potatoes		88	85	83	79	✓✓✓	- 4.7
Sandwiches		80	80	76	71	✓✓✓	- 7.5
Vegetables		34	34	34	33	✓✓	- 0.8
Ice cream, desserts and cakes		31	32	29	29	✓✓✓	- 0.7
Cheese and egg dishes and pizza		25	26	26	25	✓✓	- 4.9
Indian, Chinese and Thai meals or dishes		22	22	20	21	✓	+ 6.7
Salads		16	17	18	19	✓✓	+ 2.6
Confectionery		23	22	22	18	✓✓	- 16.0
Rice, pasta and noodles		15	15	14	15	✓✓	+ 7.6
Other food products		14	14	14	15	✓✓	+ 3.1
Fish and fish products		15	14	14	14	✓✓	0.0
Soups		10	11	10	10	✓✓	+ 3.4
Crisps, nuts and snacks		13	12	12	10	✓✓	- 18.7
Bread		9.1	9.2	8.7	8.4	✓✓	-
Fruit		8.6	8.4	8.1	8.4	✓	-
Biscuits		3.7	3.4	3.6	3.3	✓✓	-
Yoghurt		2.9	3.3	2.7	2.9	✓	-
Breakfast cereals		0.2	0.2	0.2	0.4	x	-
					£ per person per week unless otherwise specified		
Food and non-alcoholic drinks		6.98	7.21	7.33	7.72	✓✓✓	+ 5.3
Alcoholic drinks		3.71	3.73	3.60	3.54	✓✓	- 1.7
Total expenditure		10.68	10.94	10.93	11.26	✓✓✓	+ 3.0

(a) Relative standard error. 3 ticks <2.5%, 2 ticks <5%, 1 tick < 10%, no ticks <20%, 1 cross >20%
– not statistically reliable

7 Table 6.2 shows the average number of occurrences of food and drink items purchased per person per year for consumption outside the home. This is an average across the whole population and it should be remembered that in reality some people will never buy some, or all, of the items for consumption outside the home. In 2004-05 each person consumed an average of 396 items of food or drink eaten out per year, 6.7 per cent fewer than in 2003-04. Food items accounted for 57 per cent of the occurrences, alcoholic drinks 20 per cent and other drinks 24 per cent.

Table 6.2 UK average occurrences of food and drink purchased for consumption outside the home

	2001-02	2002-03	2003-04	2004-05	% change since 2003-04
				number of items per person per year	
Alcoholic drinks					
average across whole population	92	89	85	78	- 8.8
average excluding under 14's	113	108	103	94	- 9.0
Soft drinks inc. milk drinks	59	59	60	54	- 10.0
Beverages	44	42	41	40	- 0.8
Meat and meat products	36	36	38	35	- 7.6
Potatoes	28	27	27	25	- 5.5
Sandwiches	25	25	25	24	- 4.2
Confectionery	29	28	27	22	- 16.7
Ice cream, desserts and cakes	20	20	19	18	- 1.5
Vegetables	19	18	18	18	- 1.3
Other food products	19	19	19	18	- 5.5
Crisps, nuts and snacks	18	18	17	14	- 18.7
Bread	10	10	10	9	- 5.4
Cheese and egg dishes and pizza	8	9	9	9	-
Biscuits	6	6	6	6	-
Salads	5	5	5	5	-
Indian, Chinese and Thai meals or dishes	4	5	5	5	-
Fish and fish products	5	5	5	5	-
Fruit	4	4	4	4	-
Rice, pasta and noodles	4	4	4	4	-
Soups	2	3	2	2	-
Yoghurt	1	1	1	1	-
Breakfast cereals	0	0	0	0	-

– not statistically reliable

Estimated nutrient intakes from food and drink purchased for consumption outside the home

8 Table 6.3 shows nutrient intakes from food and drink purchased for consumption outside the home. In 2004-05 there was a fall in estimated intakes of all nutrients from food and drink purchased for consumption outside the home. This reflects the overall decrease in purchases of food and drink purchased for consumption outside the home out seen in tables 6.1 and 6.2. The largest decrease in nutrient intake, in percentage terms, was the 9.9 per cent fall in non-milk extrinsic sugars from 10.2 to 9.2 grams per person per day, reflecting the drop in purchases of confectionery and soft drinks for consumption outside the home.

9 The percentage of food energy derived from fat from food eaten out at 39.3 per cent showed little change on the previous year. This was significantly higher than the 37.6 per cent of food energy derived from fat from household supplies.

Table 6.3 UK energy and nutrient intakes from food and drink purchased for consumption outside the home (a)

		2001-02	2002-03	2003-04	2004-05	% change since 2003-04
		average intake per person per day				
Energy	kcal	212	210	205	191	- 6.8
	MJ	0.89	0.88	0.86	0.80	- 6.8
Energy excluding alcohol	kcal	182	182	177	165	- 6.7
Protein	g	6.2	6.2	6.1	5.8	- 4.6
Fat	g	7.9	7.9	7.7	7.2	- 6.8
Fatty acids						
Saturates	g	2.8	2.8	2.7	2.5	- 7.0
Mono-unsaturates	g	3.0	3.1	3.0	2.8	- 6.6
Poly-unsaturates	g	1.5	1.5	1.5	1.4	- 7.0
Cholesterol	mg	23.9	24.5	24.6	23.0	- 6.4
Carbohydrate (b)	g	23.0	22.8	22.1	20.6	- 7.2
Total sugars	g	12.3	12.1	11.8	10.7	- 9.0
Non-milk extrinsic sugars	g	10.6	10.5	10.2	9.2	- 9.9
Starch	g	10.7	10.7	10.4	9.8	- 5.0
Fibre (c)	g	0.96	0.94	0.92	0.89	- 3.6
Alcohol	g	4.3	4.1	3.9	3.6	- 7.7
Calcium	mg	62	62	60	56	- 5.4
Iron	mg	0.80	0.80	0.79	0.76	- 3.7
Zinc	mg	0.70	0.71	0.69	0.66	- 4.1
Magnesium	mg	25	24	23	22	- 5.1
Sodium (d)	g	0.22	0.23	0.23	0.21	- 6.6
Potassium	g	0.27	0.26	0.26	0.24	- 4.8
Thiamin	mg	0.12	0.12	0.12	0.11	- 4.0
Riboflavin	mg	0.13	0.12	0.12	0.11	- 5.2
Niacin equivalent	mg	3.5	3.5	3.4	3.3	- 4.7
Vitamin B6	mg	0.27	0.26	0.25	0.24	- 5.2
Vitamin B12	µg	0.40	0.41	0.40	0.38	- 5.3
Folate	µg	30	29	29	27	- 5.1
Vitamin C	mg	6.3	5.2	5.2	4.9	- 4.4
Vitamin A						
Retinol	µg	31	33	33	31	- 6.7
β-carotene	µg	187	141	139	139	- 0.3
Total (retinol equivalent)	µg	62	57	56	54	- 4.0
Vitamin D	µg	0.24	0.24	0.24	0.23	- 4.6
Vitamin E	mg	1.20	1.19	1.15	1.07	- 6.8
		as a percentage of total food and drink energy excluding alcohol				
Fat	%	39.1	39.3	39.4	39.3	- 0.1
Fatty acids						
Saturates	%	13.7	13.8	13.8	13.7	- 0.4
Mono-unsaturates	%	15.1	15.2	15.2	15.2	0.0
Poly-unsaturates	%	7.5	7.6	7.6	7.6	- 0.3
Carbohydrate	%	47.5	47.1	46.9	46.7	- 0.6
Non-milk extrinsic sugars	%	21.8	21.6	21.6	20.8	- 3.5
Protein	%	13.6	13.7	13.8	14.1	+ 2.2

continued

Table 6.3 continued

		2001-02	2002-03	2003-04	2004-05	% change since 2003-04
		as a percentage of weighted reference nutrient intake (e)					
Energy (f)	%	9	9	9	8	- 6.8
Energy excluding alcohol (f)	%	8	8	8	7	- 6.6
Protein	%	12	12	12	11	- 4.6
Calcium	%	8	8	8	7	- 5.4
Iron	%	7	7	7	7	- 3.6
Zinc	%	8	8	8	7	- 4.2
Magnesium	%	8	8	8	8	- 5.1
Sodium (d)	%	13	14	14	13	- 6.5
Potassium	%	8	7	7	7	- 4.8
Thiamin	%	13	13	12	12	- 3.9
Riboflavin	%	10	10	10	9	- 5.2
Niacin equivalent	%	23	23	22	21	- 4.7
Vitamin B6	%	20	19	18	17	- 5.2
Vitamin B12	%	26	26	26	24	- 5.3
Folate	%	14	14	14	13	- 5.0
Vitamin C	%	15	12	12	12	- 4.4
Vitamin A (retinol equivalent)	%	9	8	8	8	- 4.1

(a) Contributions from pharmaceutical sources are not recorded by the survey
(b) Available carbohydrate, calculated as monosaccharide equivalent
(c) As non-starch polysaccharides
(d) (i) Excludes sodium from table salt (ii) The RNI for sodium is the amount that is sufficient for 97 per cent of the population. In May 2003 the Scientific Advisory Committee on Nutrition made recommendations about the maximum amount of salt that people should be eating, i.e. that the average salt intake for adults should be no more than 6 grams per day, equivalent to 2.4 grams of sodium per day
(e) Department of Health, 'Dietary Reference Values for Food Energy and Nutrients for the United Kingdom', HMSO 1991
(f) As a percentage of Estimated Average Requirement

Intakes from 'eating out' since 1994

10 Table 6.4 shows how intakes of energy and macronutrients from eating out differ from those from household food. It shows intakes of energy, energy excluding alcohol, fat, saturated fatty acids, non-milk extrinsic sugars and alcohol from household food and drink and food and drink eaten out.

11 Figures from 1994 to 2000 are based on the National Food Survey. Whilst eating out figures from 1994 to 2000 are considered to be of poor quality due to problems with data collection the data are still of value at aggregated levels and as an indication of trends over time.

12 Figures from 2001-02 onwards are from the Expenditure and Food Survey. The annual change between 2000 and 2001-02 is less reliable than annual changes for other years due to the change in data source, particularly for eating out. The National Food Survey results for household food were adjusted to be broadly comparable to the latest results based on the Expenditure and Food Survey but the results for eating out were not adjusted.

13 Eating out accounted for 8.5 per cent of total energy intake (including alcohol) in 2004-05, compared with 9.0 per cent in 2003-04. There appeared to be a slight downward trend across the four years of data from the Expenditure and Food Survey. The apparent drop from 9.7 per cent in 2000 to 9.2 per cent in 2001-02 was probably due to the break in the series for eating out. The proportion of energy intake excluding alcohol accounted for by food and drink purchased for consumption outside the home also fell slightly each year from 2001-02 to 2004-05.

14 Fat and non-milk extrinsic sugar intakes from both household food and drink and food and drink consumed outside the home were relatively stable after 2001-02. Estimates of fat intake from eating out are lower in the Expenditure and Food Survey than in the National Food Survey (which is consistent with energy intake). The apparent drop from 10.4 per cent in 2000 was due to the break in the eating out series. Eating out accounted for 8.0 per cent of fat intake and 10.3 per cent of non-milk extrinsic sugars in 2004-05.

15 Purchases of alcohol for consumption outside the home were severely under-reported in the National Food Survey and are still under-reported on the Expenditure and Food Survey, though to a lesser extent. However the trends do indicate that alcohol intake from food and drink purchased for consumption outside the home fell from 1997 onwards.

Table 6.4 Eating out contributions to selected intakes in the UK (a)(b)

		1994	1995	1996	1997	1998	1999	2000	2001-02	2002-03	2003-04	2004-05
										average per person per day		
Energy												
eating out	kcal	250	240	255	265	260	255	230	212	210	205	191
household	kcal	2 137	2 143	2 241	2 168	2 102	2 056	2 152	2 089	2 099	2 077	2 048
% from eating out	%	10.5	10.1	10.2	10.9	11.0	11.0	9.7	9.2	9.1	9.0	8.5
Energy excluding alcohol												
eating out	kcal	230	220	235	245	242	238	214	182	182	177	165
household	kcal	2 101	2 103	2 200	2 126	2 060	2 012	2 101	2 041	2 051	2 025	1 998
% from eating out	%	9.9	9.5	9.7	10.3	10.5	10.6	9.2	8.2	8.1	8.0	7.6
Fat												
eating out	g	12	11	11	12	12	11	10	8	8	8	7
household	g	91	89	93	89	86	83	86	86	85	85	83
% from eating out	%	11.7	11.0	10.5	11.9	12.3	11.7	10.4	8.4	8.5	8.4	8.0
Saturated fatty acids												
eating out	g	5	4	5	5	5	5	4	3	3	3	3
household	g	36	36	37	35	34	33	35	34	34	34	33
% from eating out	%	11.4	11.0	10.9	11.3	11.6	12.0	10.4	7.6	7.6	7.5	7.1
Non-milk extrinsic sugars												
eating out	g	9	9	11	11	11	10	10	11	10	10	9
household	g	87	87	91	88	84	82	88	81	82	82	80
% from eating out	%	9.4	9.6	10.7	11.1	11.6	10.9	10.2	11.6	11.3	11.1	10.3
Alcohol												
eating out (c)	g	3	3	3	3	3	2	2	4	4	4	4
household	g	5	6	6	6	6	6	7	7	7	7	7
% from eating out	%	36.5	33.7	31.9	32.6	30.1	27.6	24.2	38.0	37.2	34.7	33.5

(a) National Food Survey data 1994 to 2000, Expenditure and Food Survey data 2001-02 onwards
(b) Household estimates from the National Food Survey have been adjusted to be comparable with household estimates from the Expenditure and Food Survey but eating out estimates have not been adjusted.
(c) Consumption of alocoholic drinks outside the home was severely under-reported in the National Food Survey.

Contributions to intakes by type of food and drink purchased for consumption outside the home

16 Table 6.5 shows how different types of food and drink purchased for consumption outside the home contributed to intakes of selected macronutrients and micronutrients in 2004-05. Most of the intake of energy and nutrients from eating out was in the form of meat and meat products, sandwiches, potatoes and potato products, and alcoholic drinks. Soft drinks, confectionery and alcoholic drinks were the main sources of non-milk extrinsic sugars. Meat and meat products, and sandwiches, were the main sources of sodium.

Table 6.5 Intakes by different types of food and drink purchased for consumption outside the home in 2004-05

	Energy	Fat	Saturated fatty acids	Calcium	Iron	Non-milk extrinsic sugars	Sodium	Folate	Vitamin C	β-carotene	Vitamin A (Retinol equiv.)
									average per person per day		
	kcal	grams	grams	mg	mg	grams	mg	µg	mg	µg	µg
Indian, Chinese and Thai meals or dishes	4	0.2	0.0	1	0.1	0.1	9.6	0.2	0.1	4.3	0.9
Meat and meat products	30	1.8	0.7	8	0.2	0.0	66.6	2.3	0.2	31.5	15.8
Fish and fish products	4	0.2	0.0	1	0.0	0.0	5.0	0.4	0.0	0.1	0.5
Cheese & egg dishes & pizza	8	0.5	0.2	5	0.1	0.0	12.6	2.5	0.1	5.4	5.4
Potatoes	20	0.8	0.1	1	0.1	0.0	3.4	5.4	1.7	0.5	0.6
Vegetables	4	0.1	0.0	2	0.1	0.0	9.6	1.8	0.3	52.4	9.1
Salads	1	0.1	0.0	1	0.0	0.0	2.0	0.7	0.4	18.9	3.5
Rice, pasta and noodles	3	0.1	0.0	0	0.0	0.0	1.1	0.1	0.0	0.3	0.1
Soups	1	0.0	0.0	0	0.0	0.0	6.6	0.3	0.0	0.2	0.0
Breakfast cereals	0	0.0	0.0	0	0.0	0.0	0.3	0.1	0.0	0.0	0.0
Fruit	1	0.0	0.0	0	0.0	0.0	0.0	0.1	0.2	0.9	0.2
Yoghurt	0	0.0	0.0	1	0.0	0.0	0.3	0.0	0.0	0.0	0.1
Bread	4	0.2	0.1	1	0.0	0.0	7.4	0.3	0.0	1.1	1.8
Sandwiches	21	1.0	0.3	12	0.1	0.0	44.6	2.4	0.2	13.0	6.8
Other food products	4	0.3	0.1	2	0.0	0.1	7.6	0.3	0.1	3.9	2.2
Beverages	2	0.1	0.0	2	0.0	0.1	1.2	0.4	0.0	0.4	0.6
Soft drinks including milk	15	0.1	0.0	5	0.0	3.6	3.3	0.6	1.0	0.8	0.7
Alcoholic drinks	35	0.0	0.0	6	0.0	2.4	6.5	8.2	0.3	0.2	0.0
Confectionery	11	0.4	0.2	3	0.0	1.7	2.3	0.1	0.0	0.6	0.3
Ice cream, desserts & cakes	13	0.7	0.3	3	0.0	0.8	9.9	0.4	0.1	4.0	5.3
Biscuits	2	0.1	0.0	1	0.0	0.1	0.9	0.1	0.0	0.1	0.0
Crisps, nuts and snacks	7	0.5	0.2	0	0.0	0.1	10.5	0.5	0.1	0.4	0.1
All Food & Drink Eaten Out	**191**	**7.2**	**2.5**	**56**	**0.8**	**9.2**	**211.5**	**27.2**	**4.9**	**138.9**	**53.9**
	as a percentage of total intake per person per day from food and drink purchased for consumption outside the home										
	%	%	%	%	%	%	%	%	%	%	%
Indian, Chinese and Thai meals or dishes	2	3	2	2	9	1	5	1	1	3	2
Meat and meat Products	16	24	27	14	21	0	31	8	4	23	29
Fish and fish products	2	3	2	2	2	0	2	1	0	0	1
Cheese & egg dishes & pizza	4	7	7	9	7	0	6	9	3	4	10
Potatoes	10	12	5	2	9	0	2	20	35	0	1
Vegetables	2	2	1	4	7	1	5	7	7	38	17
Salads	1	1	1	2	2	0	1	3	9	14	6
Rice, pasta and noodles	1	1	0	1	2	0	1	0	0	0	0
Soups	0	0	0	0	1	0	3	1	0	0	0
Breakfast cereals	0	0	0	0	0	0	0	0	0	0	0
Fruit	0	0	0	0	0	0	0	0	5	1	0
Yoghurt	0	0	0	1	0	0	0	0	0	0	0
Bread	2	3	4	3	2	0	3	1	0	1	3
Sandwiches	11	14	12	21	15	0	21	9	4	9	13
Other food products	2	5	6	3	2	1	4	1	2	3	4
Beverages	1	1	2	4	2	1	1	1	1	0	1
Soft drinks including milk	8	1	1	9	1	39	2	2	19	1	1
Alcoholic drinks	18	0	0	10	6	26	3	30	7	0	0
Confectionery	6	5	9	5	3	18	1	0	0	0	1
Ice cream, desserts & cakes	7	10	13	6	5	9	5	2	1	3	10
Biscuits	1	2	2	1	1	2	0	0	0	0	0
Crisps, nuts and snacks	4	6	7	1	2	1	5	2	1	0	0

Chapter 7 Geographic Comparisons

Headlines

Over the three year period April 2002 to March 2005,

in the countries of the UK,

- quantities of fruit and vegetables (excluding fresh and processed potatoes) purchased for the household were highest in England and lowest in Northern Ireland

- quantities of fresh and processed potatoes purchased for the household were highest in Northern Ireland and lowest in Scotland

- Scottish households purchased the most soft drinks

- expenditure on alcoholic drinks (i.e. including both household and eating out purchases) was highest in England and lowest in Northern Ireland

in the regions of England,

- household purchases of vegetables (excluding fresh and processed potatoes) were lowest in the North West of England and highest in the South West of England

- the North East had the lowest household purchases of fruit and the East had the highest

- expenditure on alcoholic drinks (i.e. including both household and eating out purchases) was highest in Yorkshire and The Humber and lowest in the East

- when eating out, households in London purchased the most Indian, Chinese and Thai meals, and Yorkshire and The Humber purchased the most fish products and fresh and processed potatoes

- eating out expenditure as a percentage of overall food and drink spending was 38 per cent in London and 30 per cent in the East compared with 33 per cent across England as whole

[1] This section presents estimates for the four countries of the United Kingdom and the nine Government Office Regions of England. To improve reliability, the figures shown in the tables are all averages of the estimates for 2002-03, 2003-04 and 2004-05. The total sample size for the three years is given at the top of each column as an indication of the reliability of the figures. Differences in relative prices and household income should also be born in mind when interpreting the data.

[2] Although the figures for the countries and regions are averages for a three year period, useful comparisons can still be made with the annual 2004-05 averages for the UK as a whole.

[3] The purchases and expenditure tables contain data from both household food and drink and eating out. The energy and nutrient intake tables not only include the combined intakes from

food brought into the home and eaten out but also the contributions from soft drinks, alcoholic drinks and confectionery.

4 For a more detailed breakdown of the data in respect of the countries and regions please refer to the datasets which are published on the Defra website at: http://statistics.defra.gov.uk/esg/publications/efs/datasets/default.asp

United Kingdom countries

Household

5 Tables 7.1 and 7.2 show that there was little variation between the countries in household purchases of milk and cream, all meat and meat products, total cereals, beverages and confectionery. For these products the ratio of purchases per person in the highest purchasing country to that in the lowest purchasing country was 1.2 or less. Households in England purchased the most cheese, fish, vegetables (excluding fresh and processed potatoes) and fruit, and households in Northern Ireland purchased the least. Households in Northern Ireland purchased more than one and a half times the quantity of fresh and processed potatoes that households in Scotland purchased. The quantity of alcoholic drinks purchased for the household was highest in Wales, over one and a half times more than in Northern Ireland. However, household expenditure on alcoholic drinks was highest in Scotland. Total expenditure on household food and drink varied little between countries.

Eating Out

6 English households had the highest eating out purchases of fish and fish products and beverages, over one and a half times more than in Northern Ireland. The quantity of vegetables purchased for consumption outside the home was also highest in England but was lowest in Scotland. Households in Scotland purchased over one and a half times more sandwiches to eat outside the home than households in Northern Ireland. Northern Irish households purchased nearly one and a half times more ice cream, desserts and cakes when eating out than Welsh households. Scottish households purchased the most soft drinks whilst English households purchased the largest quantity of alcoholic drink for consumption outside the home. There was little variation between the countries in expenditure on food and drink purchased for consumption outside the home, which generally represented just under a third of the overall expenditure on food and drink.

Intakes

7 Table 7.3 shows that intakes of energy and many nutrients were higher in England and Wales than in Northern Ireland and Scotland. Households in England had the highest intakes of vitamins A and C. The higher intake of vitamin C reflects the higher quantities of vegetables (excluding fresh and processed potatoes) and fruit purchased by English households. The percentage contribution of fat to energy intake was highest in Wales and lowest in Scotland whereas for carbohydrate the percentage contribution was highest in Scotland and Northern Ireland and lowest in Wales. The percentage contribution of protein to energy intake was highest in England and lowest in Northern Ireland.

Table 7.1 Highest and lowest countries (average April 2002 to March 2005)

	Lowest	Highest	Ratio of lowest to highest
Household purchases			
Milk and cream	England	Northern Ireland	1.1
Cheese	Northern Ireland	England	1.5
Carcase meat	Scotland	Wales	1.2
Other meat and meat products	Northern Ireland	Wales	1.1
Fish	Northern Ireland	England	1.4
Fats and oils	Scotland	Wales	1.2
Sugar and preserves	Northern Ireland	Wales	1.3
Fresh and processed potatoes	Scotland	Northern Ireland	1.6
Vegetables (excluding potatoes)	Northern Ireland	England	1.4
Fruit	Northern Ireland	England	1.3
Total cereals	Wales	Northern Ireland	1.1
Beverages	Northern Ireland	England	1.2
Soft drinks	England	Scotland	1.3
Confectionery	England	Wales	1.2
Eating out purchases			
Indian, Chinese and Thai meals or dishes	Scotland	England	1.3
Meat and meat products	Scotland	Wales	1.2
Fish and fish products	Northern Ireland	England	1.6
Cheese and egg dishes and pizza	Northern Ireland	England	1.4
Potatoes	Scotland	Northern Ireland	1.3
Vegetables (excluding potatoes)	Scotland	England	1.8
Sandwiches	Northern Ireland	Scotland	1.7
Ice creams, desserts and cakes	Wales	Northern Ireland	1.4
Beverages	Northern Ireland	England	1.5
Soft drinks including milk	England	Scotland	1.3
Confectionery	England	Northern Ireland	1.4
Household expenditure			
Total all food and drink excluding alcohol	Wales	Scotland	1.1
Total alcoholic drinks	Northern Ireland	Scotland	1.4
Total all food and drink	Wales	Scotland	1.1
Eating out expenditure			
Total all food and drink excluding alcohol	Wales	England	1.2
Total alcoholic drinks	Scotland	England	1.2
Total all food and drink	Wales	England	1.2

Table 7.2 Selected foods by country (average April 2002 to March 2005)

		England	Wales	Scotland	Northern Ireland
Number of households in sample		16 240	1 075	1 724	1 734
Average age of HRP		52	52	51	50
Average number of adults per household		1.9	1.8	1.8	1.9
Average number of children per household		0.5	0.6	0.5	0.6
Average gross weekly household income (£)		581	475	510	482
Household purchases		*grams per person per week unless otherwise stated*			
Milk and cream	ml	1 987	2 065	2 030	2 141
Cheese		114	99	109	74
Carcase meat		229	242	202	242
Other meat and meat products		820	885	849	804
Fish		160	147	138	111
Eggs	no.	1.6	1.6	1.7	1.5
Fats and oils		187	200	167	183
Sugar and preserves		138	158	132	119
Fresh and processed potatoes		838	964	795	1 268
Vegetables excluding potatoes		1 126	1 064	896	831
Fruit		1 218	1 054	1 060	929
Total cereals		1 616	1 596	1 646	1 718
Beverages	ml	58	51	49	47
Soft drinks (a)	ml	1 787	2 045	2 251	1 824
Alcoholic drinks	ml	769	780	747	497
Confectionery		126	151	146	135
Eating out purchases		*grams per person per week unless otherwise stated*			
Indian, Chinese and Thai meals or dishes		22	19	16	19
Meat and meat products		94	105	84	104
Fish and fish products		14	13	13	9
Cheese and egg dishes and pizza		26	23	21	19
Potatoes		82	94	76	98
Vegetables excluding potatoes		35	34	20	27
Sandwiches		77	60	82	47
Ice creams, desserts and cakes		30	24	31	35
Beverages		147	126	128	97
Soft drinks including milk	ml	359	363	458	426
Alcoholic drinks	ml	680	669	507	522
Confectionery		20	22	26	28
Household expenditure		*pence per person per week*			
Milk and cream		153	151	149	157
Cheese		60	48	58	41
Carcase meat		110	110	105	129
Other meat and meat products		370	379	408	418
Fish		98	81	87	70
Eggs		18	16	18	16
Fats and oils		37	38	36	37
Sugar and preserves		16	17	16	15
Fresh and processed potatoes		98	107	110	137
Vegetables excluding potatoes		182	156	149	135
Fruit		167	142	146	127
Total cereals		368	341	390	406
Beverages		43	37	38	35
All other foods		119	117	122	111
Soft drinks		76	78	106	92
Alcoholic drinks		262	239	273	198
Confectionery		79	91	92	79
Total all food and drink excluding alcohol		1 995	1 910	2 030	2 007
Total all food and drink		2 257	2 149	2 303	2 205
Eating out expenditure		*pence per person per week*			
Total all food and drink excluding alcohol		754	636	686	738
Total alcoholic drinks		372	330	300	325
Total all food and drink		1 126	966	987	1 063

(a) Converted to unconcentrated equivalent by applying a factor of 5 to concentrated and low calorie concentrated soft drinks

Table 7.3 Energy and nutrient intakes by country (average April 2002 to March 2005) (a)

		England	Wales	Scotland	Northern Ireland
Number of households in sample		16 240	1 075	1 724	1 734
Average age of HRP		52	52	51	50
Average number of adults per household		1.9	1.8	1.8	1.9
Average number of children per household		0.5	0.6	0.5	0.6
Average gross weekly household income (£)		581	475	510	482
		\multicolumn{4}{c}{intake per person per day}
Energy	kcal	2 320	2 326	2 179	2 258
	MJ	9.8	9.8	9.2	9.5
Energy intake excluding alcohol	kcal	2 242	2 248	2 109	2 195
Protein	g	78.8	78.6	73.7	76.2
Fat	g	94	96	87	91
Fatty acids:					
Saturates	g	36.7	37.6	34.4	36.2
Mono-unsaturates	g	34.0	34.8	31.7	33.2
Poly-unsaturates	g	16.5	16.8	15.3	15.7
Cholesterol	mg	261	264	247	249
Carbohydrate (b)	g	289	286	274	285
Total sugars	g	138	138	130	132
Non-milk extrinsic sugars	g	93	95	89	89
Starch	g	151	148	143	153
Fibre (c)	g	14.5	14.1	13.3	14.1
Alcohol	g	11	11	10	9
Calcium	mg	1 014	997	936	977
Iron	mg	12.3	12.0	11.3	11.9
Zinc	mg	9.3	9.2	8.7	8.9
Magnesium	mg	286	279	265	273
Sodium (d)	g	3.07	3.15	2.70	3.01
Potassium	g	3.21	3.15	2.88	3.15
Thiamin	mg	1.71	1.67	1.56	1.69
Riboflavin	mg	2.01	1.97	1.85	1.93
Niacin equivalent	mg	34.74	34.63	32.28	33.46
Vitamin B6	mg	2.48	2.49	2.27	2.53
Vitamin B12	µg	6.49	6.57	6.10	5.94
Folate	µg	296	284	265	283
Vitamin C	mg	73	66	68	68
Vitamin A:					
Retinol	µg	547	522	495	452
β-carotene	µg	2 031	1 967	1 742	1 839
Retinol equivalent	µg	892	856	790	765
Vitamin D	µg	3.37	3.40	3.01	3.12
Vitamin E	mg	12.34	12.56	11.37	11.75
		\multicolumn{4}{c}{percentage contributions of macronutrients to energy intake excluding alcohol}
Fat	%	37.6	38.3	37.3	37.4
Fatty acids:					
Saturates	%	14.7	15.0	14.7	14.8
Mono-unsaturates	%	13.7	13.9	13.5	13.6
Poly-unsaturates	%	6.6	6.7	6.5	6.4
Carbohydrate	%	48.4	47.8	48.7	48.7
Non-milk extrinsic sugars	%	15.5	15.9	15.8	15.2
Protein	%	14.1	14.0	14.0	13.9

continued

Table 7.3 continued

		England	Wales	Scotland	Northern Ireland
		\multicolumn{4}{r}{as a percentage of weighted reference nutrient intake (e)}
Energy (f)	%	100	98	95	97
Energy excluding alcohol (f)	%	97	95	92	94
Protein	%	157	156	140	155
Calcium	%	134	130	114	128
Iron	%	107	350	95	104
Zinc	%	106	104	95	103
Magnesium	%	97	95	87	96
Sodium (d)	%	230	224	206	182
Potassium	%	91	89	80	90
Thiamin	%	181	179	162	180
Riboflavin	%	159	155	138	155
Niacin equivalent	%	228	225	202	221
Vitamin B6	%	183	180	161	182
Vitamin B12	%	418	436	375	416
Folate	%	138	134	126	141
Vitamin C	%	166	156	163	177
Vitamin A (retinol equivalent)	%	125	124	111	127

(a) Contributions from pharmaceutical sources are not recorded by the survey
(b) Available carbohydrate, calculated as monosaccharide equivalent
(c) As non-starch polysaccharides
(d) (i) Excludes sodium from table salt (ii) The RNI for sodium is the amount that is sufficient for 97 per cent of the population. In May 2003 the Scientific Advisory Committee on Nutrition made recommendations about the maximum amount of salt that people should be eating, i.e. that the average salt intake for adults should be no more than 6 grams per day, equivalent to 2.4 grams of sodium per day
(e) Department of Health, 'Dietary Reference Values for Food Energy and Nutrients for the United Kingdom', HMSO 1991
(f) As a percentage of Estimated Average Requirement

England regions

Household

8   Tables 7.4 and 7.5 show that there was little regional difference in the quantities of household purchases of carcase meat, fish, fats and oils, vegetables and cereals. The largest regional differences were for purchases of alcoholic drinks and confectionery. Households in the North West purchased more than one and a half times the quantity of alcoholic drinks purchased by London households. London households purchased the lowest quantities of most types of food and drink apart from carcase meat, fish and fruit. Households in the North East purchased the least carcase meat and fruit but the most meat products, soft drinks and confectionery. Purchases of vegetables (excluding fresh and processed potatoes) and fruit were highest in the South West and the East respectively.

9   Households in the Yorkshire and The Humber region spent 9.1 per cent less than the average for UK households on food and drink purchases for the home whereas households in the South East spent 5.6 per cent more than the UK figure of £23.05 per person per week. For the UK as a whole 12 per cent of the household food and drink budget was spent on alcoholic drinks. In the North West 13 per cent of the budget was spent on alcoholic drinks compared with 11 per cent in the East.

Eating out

10 There was a large regional difference in the quantity of Indian, Chinese and Thai meals eaten out. The quantity purchased per person per week in London was over two and a half times the quantity purchased in the North East. London also had the highest purchases of cheese, egg and pizza dishes, sandwiches and ice creams, desserts and cakes eaten out. Yorkshire and The Humber showed the highest purchases of fish and fish products, fresh and processed potatoes and alcoholic drinks purchased for consumption outside the home. Combining household and 'eating out' purchases of alcoholic drinks it was households in the North East that purchased the most alcoholic drinks and households in London that purchased the least.

11 London spent the most on food and non-alcoholic drinks for consumption outside the home and the North East spent the least. Yorkshire and The Humber spent the most on alcoholic drinks for consumption outside the home and the East spent the least. When comparing eating out expenditure with the UK figure of £11.26 per person per week, households in the West Midlands spent 14 per cent less (£9.71) whereas households in London spent 21 per cent more (£13.60).

12 There was a wider variation than at country level in eating out expenditure as a percentage of overall food and drink spending with 38 per cent of the total being spent on eating out in London compared with 30 per cent in the East. For the United Kingdom as a whole, eating out expenditure represented 33 per cent of the total.

Intakes

13 Table 7.6 compares the energy and nutrient intakes across the regions. Energy intake and the intakes of most nutrients were lowest in London. Intakes of energy, protein, fat, carbohydrate, cholesterol, alcohol and some minerals and vitamins were highest in the North West. Intakes of fibre, iron, riboflavin, folate and vitamin A were highest in the South West. The intake of vitamin C was lowest in the North East and highest in the East, South East and South West which reflects the differences between the regions in purchases of fruit.

14 There was very little variation across the regions in the percentage contributions of macronutrients to energy intake (excluding alcohol).

Table 7.4 Highest and lowest regions (average April 2002 to March 2005)

	Lowest	Highest	Ratio of lowest to highest
Household purchases			
Milk and cream	London	South West	1.3
Cheese	London	South West	1.4
Carcase meat	North East	South West	1.2
Other meat and meat products	London	North East	1.4
Fish	West Midlands	East	1.2
Fats and oils	London	South West	1.1
Sugar and preserves	London	South West	1.3
Fresh and processed potatoes	London	West Midlands	1.4
Vegetables (excluding potatoes)	North West	South West	1.2
Fruit	North East	East	1.4
Total cereals	London	North East	1.1
Beverages	London	East Midlands	1.4
Soft drinks	London	North East	1.3
Confectionery	London	North East	1.6
Eating out purchases			
Indian, Chinese and Thai meals or dishes	North East	London	2.6
Meat and meat products	West Midlands	North West	1.2
Fish and fish products	West Midlands	Yorkshire and The Humber	1.5
Cheese and egg dishes and pizza	South East	London	1.4
Potatoes	South East	Yorkshire and The Humber	1.3
Vegetables (excluding potatoes)	North East	East Midlands	1.4
Sandwiches	South West	London	1.4
Ice creams, desserts and cakes	West Midlands	London	1.3
Beverages	North East	East Midlands	1.4
Soft drinks including milk	South West	North East	1.5
Confectionery	South West	North East	1.4
Household expenditure			
Total all food and drink excluding alcohol	Yorkshire and The Humber	South East	1.2
Total alcoholic drinks	London	North West	1.3
Total all food and drink	Yorkshire and The Humber	South East	1.2
Eating out expenditure			
Total all food and drink excluding alcohol	North East	London	1.6
Total alcoholic drinks	East	Yorkshire and The Humber	1.5
Total all food and drink	West Midlands	London	1.4

Table 7.5 Selected foods by region (average April 2002 to March 2005)

		England	North East	North West	Yorkshire and The Humber	East Midlands
Number of households in sample		16 240	886	2 211	1 723	1 408
Average age of HRP		52	52	51	52	51
Average number of adults per household		1.9	1.8	1.9	1.9	1.9
Average number of children per household		0.5	0.5	0.5	0.5	0.5
Average gross weekly household income (£)		581	444	520	511	546
Household purchases		\multicolumn{5}{r}{*grams per person per week unless otherwise stated*}
Milk and cream	ml	1 987	2 042	2 060	1 964	2 159
Cheese		114	102	109	104	124
Carcase meat		229	213	228	228	224
Other meat and meat products		820	954	895	828	855
Fish		160	168	156	161	155
Eggs	no.	1.6	1.7	1.6	1.6	1.6
Fats and oils		187	187	185	180	186
Sugar and preserves		138	142	139	138	145
Fresh and processed potatoes		838	915	853	851	908
Vegetables excluding potatoes		1 126	1 003	994	1 051	1 154
Fruit		1 218	963	1 090	1 108	1 183
Total cereals		1 616	1 695	1 642	1 598	1 686
Beverages	ml	58	55	58	57	65
Soft drinks (a)	ml	1 787	2 006	1 804	1 760	1 937
Alcoholic drinks	ml	769	885	916	843	801
Confectionery		126	149	131	133	138
Eating out purchases		\multicolumn{5}{r}{*grams per person per week unless otherwise stated*}
Indian, Chinese and Thai meals or dishes		22	12	20	20	19
Meat and meat products		94	95	104	98	101
Fish and fish products		14	15	13	18	14
Cheese and egg dishes and pizza		26	29	24	27	26
Fresh and processed potatoes		82	92	89	93	92
Vegetables excluding potatoes		35	32	34	40	44
Sandwiches		77	73	81	84	78
Ice creams, desserts and cakes		30	27	28	30	28
Beverages	ml	147	125	143	141	171
Soft drinks including milk	ml	359	422	386	366	380
Alcoholic drinks	ml	680	890	835	895	692
Confectionery		20	24	23	21	23
Household expenditure		\multicolumn{5}{r}{*pence per person per week*}
Milk and cream		153	148	154	143	162
Cheese		60	49	54	50	61
Carcase meat		110	93	110	103	105
Other meat and meat products		370	377	390	347	371
Fish		98	93	85	98	89
Eggs		18	16	17	16	17
Fats and oils		37	35	36	34	35
Sugar and preserves		16	14	15	15	16
Fresh and processed potatoes		98	111	102	97	103
Vegetables excluding potatoes		182	139	155	154	167
Fruit		167	124	141	140	150
Total cereals		368	376	368	353	374
Beverages		43	39	42	41	45
All other foods		119	104	118	101	113
Soft drinks		76	77	77	71	76
Alcoholic drinks		262	237	297	253	261
Confectionery		79	85	79	79	86
Total all food and drink excluding alcohol		1 995	1 880	1 941	1 841	1 970
Total all food and drink		2 257	2 117	2 239	2 094	2 231
Eating out expenditure		\multicolumn{5}{r}{*pence per person per week*}
Total all food and drink excluding alcohol		754	603	719	688	731
Total alcoholic drinks		372	394	423	433	385
Total all food and drink		1 126	998	1 142	1 121	1 117

(a) Converted to unconcentrated equivalent by applying a factor of 5 to concentrated and low calorie concentrated soft drinks

continued

Table 7.5 continued

		West Midlands	East	London	South East	South West
Number of households in sample		1 670	1 876	1 875	2 705	1 886
Average age of HRP		52	52	50	52	54
Average number of adults per household		1.9	1.9	1.9	1.9	1.8
Average number of children per household		0.6	0.5	0.6	0.5	0.4
Average gross weekly household income (£)		520	619	745	667	541
Household purchases		*grams per person per week unless otherwise stated*				
Milk and cream	ml	1 962	1 999	1 680	2 004	2 180
Cheese		109	123	97	124	131
Carcase meat		239	222	223	232	247
Other meat and meat products		823	831	700	804	803
Fish		148	171	171	160	151
Eggs	no.	1.6	1.6	1.7	1.6	1.7
Fats and oils		195	188	178	188	197
Sugar and preserves		148	138	121	133	154
Fresh and processed potatoes		935	862	657	815	881
Vegetables excluding potatoes		1 122	1 194	1 134	1 190	1 234
Fruit		1 064	1 360	1 279	1 355	1 357
Total cereals		1 633	1 629	1 499	1 599	1 669
Beverages	ml	61	59	46	61	63
Soft drinks (a)	ml	1 888	1 905	1 588	1 760	1 657
Alcoholic drinks	ml	728	747	573	748	803
Confectionery		121	136	93	124	136
Eating out purchases		*grams per person per week unless otherwise stated*				
Indian, Chinese and Thai meals or dishes		20	19	31	27	15
Meat and meat products		85	87	98	88	92
Fish and fish products		12	15	15	13	15
Cheese and egg dishes and pizza		25	26	32	24	24
Potatoes		83	79	77	71	77
Vegetables excluding potatoes		33	33	34	32	40
Sandwiches		69	71	92	74	64
Ice creams, desserts and cakes		26	30	33	32	32
Beverages	ml	133	151	146	156	149
Soft drinks including milk	ml	336	342	406	329	289
Alcoholic drinks	ml	665	542	560	586	640
Confectionery		20	18	18	18	18
Household expenditure		*pence per person per week*				
Milk and cream		144	158	135	163	168
Cheese		56	67	56	70	70
Carcase meat		111	109	112	115	122
Other meat and meat products		361	394	339	387	367
Fish		83	111	111	108	91
Eggs		17	18	20	19	19
Fats and oils		36	37	35	40	41
Sugar and preserves		16	16	16	18	19
Fresh and processed potatoes		107	102	83	97	98
Vegetables excluding potatoes		164	197	208	213	195
Fruit		139	187	190	200	189
Total cereals		346	384	356	385	377
Beverages		42	43	35	47	49
All other foods		109	124	124	133	130
Soft drinks		76	81	82	76	68
Alcoholic drinks		234	252	232	282	287
Confectionery		74	84	64	83	86
Total all food and drink excluding alcohol		1 882	2 113	1 965	2 152	2 087
Total all food and drink		2 116	2 365	2 197	2 434	2 373
Eating out expenditure		*pence per person per week*				
Total all food and drink excluding alcohol		628	713	965	802	703
Total alcoholic drinks		344	297	395	342	344
Total all food and drink		971	1 011	1 360	1 144	1 048

(a) Converted to unconcentrated equivalent by applying a factor of 5 to concentrated and low calorie concentrated soft drinks

Table 7.6 Energy and nutrient intakes by region (average April 2002 to March 2005) (a)

		England	North East	North West	Yorkshire and The Humber	East Midlands	West Midlands	East	London	South East	South West
Number of households in sample		16 240	886	2 211	1 723	1 408	1 670	1 876	1 875	2 705	1 886
Average age of HRP		52	52	51	52	51	52	52	50	52	54
Average number of adults per household		1.9	1.8	1.9	1.9	1.9	1.9	1.9	1.9	1.9	1.8
Average number of children per household		0.5	0.5	0.5	0.5	0.5	0.6	0.5	0.6	0.5	0.4
Average gross weekly household income (£)		581	444	520	511	546	520	619	745	667	541
											intake per person per day
Energy	kcal	2 320	2 372	2 445	2 262	2 361	2 266	2 309	2 092	2 274	2 369
	MJ	9.8	10.0	10.3	9.5	9.9	9.5	9.7	8.8	9.6	10.0
Energy excluding alcohol	kcal	2 242	2 286	2 353	2 177	2 279	2 192	2 238	2 028	2 198	2 286
Protein	g	78.8	79.8	84.3	76.6	79.9	76.2	78.1	71.5	77.3	79.9
Fat	g	94	97	99	91	95	91	94	84	93	97
Fatty acids:											
Saturates	g	36.7	38.5	38.3	35.8	37.5	35.6	36.9	31.2	36.6	38.3
Mono-unsaturates	g	34.0	35.4	36.5	33.2	34.5	33.4	34.2	30.8	33.7	34.9
Poly-unsaturates	g	16.5	16.7	17.5	16.0	16.6	16.2	16.6	16.2	16.5	16.7
Cholesterol	mg	261	269	276	258	262	253	263	242	259	271
Carbohydrate (b)	g	289	292	300	280	295	284	287	263	280	293
Total sugars	g	138	140	137	134	142	133	140	120	136	143
Non-milk extrinsic sugars	g	93	98	93	91	96	91	94	79	90	94
Starch	g	151	151	163	146	152	150	147	143	144	150
Fibre (c)	g	14.5	14.0	14.8	14.0	14.7	14.1	14.8	13.5	14.5	15.3
Alcohol	g	11	12	13	12	12	11	10	9	11	12
Calcium	mg	1 014	1 010	1 028	967	1 048	977	1 001	854	990	1 039
Iron	mg	12.3	12.1	12.6	11.8	12.5	11.8	12.3	11.0	12.1	12.7
Zinc	mg	9.3	9.4	9.8	9.0	9.5	9.0	9.2	8.4	9.1	9.5
Magnesium	mg	286	284	298	277	291	275	286	258	286	297
Sodium (d)	g	3.07	3.19	3.24	2.95	3.12	2.93	3.03	2.53	3.00	3.07
Potassium	g	3.21	3.16	3.36	3.09	3.27	3.10	3.20	2.84	3.18	3.32
Thiamin	mg	1.71	1.66	1.76	1.64	1.74	1.64	1.69	1.50	1.68	1.76
Riboflavin	mg	2.01	1.98	2.04	1.94	2.05	1.91	1.99	1.73	1.99	2.09
Niacin equivalent	mg	34.74	35.36	37.41	34.13	35.16	33.60	34.51	31.46	34.20	35.25
Vitamin B6	mg	2.48	2.49	2.60	2.44	2.52	2.44	2.47	2.19	2.41	2.54
Vitamin B12	μg	6.49	6.77	6.72	6.47	6.51	6.02	6.51	5.79	6.36	6.59
Folate	μg	296	283	291	285	299	284	297	267	294	309
Vitamin C	mg	73	66	72	68	74	68	77	73	77	77
Vitamin A:											
Retinol	μg	547	554	518	539	538	485	557	483	561	587
β-carotene	μg	2 031	1 917	1 972	1 876	2 083	1 906	2 070	1 781	2 047	2 124
Retinol equivalent	μg	892	880	852	858	893	809	909	784	909	947
Vitamin D	μg	3.37	3.31	3.49	3.21	3.41	3.28	3.40	2.95	3.30	3.42
Vitamin E	mg	12.34	12.27	13.66	11.88	12.52	12.29	12.48	11.86	12.21	12.55

continued

Table 7.6 continued

		England	North East	North West	Yorkshire and The Humber	East Midlands	West Midlands	East	London	South East	South West
Fat	%	37.6	38.2	37.9	37.7	37.5	37.6	37.9	37.3	38.2	38.0
Fatty acids:											
Saturates	%	14.7	15.1	14.6	14.8	14.8	14.6	14.8	13.9	15.0	15.1
Mono-unsaturates	%	13.7	13.9	13.9	13.7	13.6	13.7	13.8	13.7	13.8	13.7
Poly-unsaturates	%	6.6	6.6	6.7	6.6	6.5	6.7	6.7	7.2	6.8	6.6
Carbohydrate	%	48.4	47.8	47.8	48.2	48.5	48.5	48.2	48.6	47.7	48.0
Non-milk extrinsic sugars	%	15.5	16.0	14.8	15.7	15.8	15.6	15.7	14.6	15.4	15.4
Protein	%	14.1	14.0	14.3	14.1	14.0	13.9	14.0	14.1	14.1	14.0
		as a percentage of weighted reference nutrient intake (e)									
Energy (f)	%	100	102	105	97	101	97	99	89	98	102
Energy excluding alcohol (f)	%	97	99	101	93	98	94	96	87	95	98
Protein	%	157	158	166	151	157	150	153	141	152	155
Calcium	%	134	132	134	126	136	127	130	112	130	135
Iron	%	107	105	927	104	108	103	107	95	106	112
Zinc	%	106	106	111	102	107	102	104	95	103	108
Magnesium	%	97	97	101	94	98	93	96	88	97	100
Sodium (d)	%	230	192	196	178	187	176	182	153	181	183
Potassium	%	91	89	95	87	92	88	90	81	90	92
Thiamin	%	181	179	188	175	185	176	181	160	180	188
Riboflavin	%	159	157	161	153	161	150	156	137	157	164
Niacin equivalent	%	228	230	242	221	227	217	222	203	222	228
Vitamin B6	%	183	184	191	179	185	179	180	161	177	185
Vitamin B12	%	418	441	438	420	423	392	421	378	413	422
Folate	%	138	135	139	136	142	136	141	128	141	146
Vitamin C	%	166	154	168	159	173	160	181	172	180	179
Vitamin A (retinol equivalent)	%	125	128	123	124	129	117	131	114	132	136

(a) Contributions from pharmaceutical sources are not recorded by the survey
(b) Available carbohydrate, calculated as monosaccharide equivalent
(c) As non-starch polysaccharides
(d) (i) Excludes sodium from table salt (ii) The RNI for sodium is the amount that is sufficient for 97 per cent of the population. In May 2003 the Scientific Advisory Committee on Nutrition made recommendations about the maximum amount of salt that people should be eating, i.e. that the average salt intake for adults should be no more than 6 grams per day, equivalent to 2.4 grams of sodium per day
(e) Department of Health, 'Dietary Reference Values for Food Energy and Nutrients for the United Kingdom', HMSO 1991
(f) As a percentage of Estimated Average Requirement

Chapter 8 Demographic Comparisons

Headlines

Over the three year period April 2002 to March 2005,

- household members in the lowest income quintile had the lowest intakes of alcohol but also the lowest intakes of vitamin C

- adult only households spent 7.2 per cent more than the UK average on food and drink eaten at home and 25 per cent more on eating out

- members of households where the Household Reference Person was aged under thirty spent 43 per cent of their food and drink budget on eating out while the "75 and over" group spent only 19 per cent of their food and drink budget on eating out

- intakes of most vitamins and minerals were lowest in households where the Household Reference Person ceased full time education at the age of 16

- the percentage of food energy derived from saturated fatty acids decreased as the age at which the Household Reference Person left full-time education increased

- household purchases of vegetables were lower in households where the Household Reference Person was classified as "Never worked and long-term unemployed" than in the households where the Household Reference Person was in employment

1. This section contains comparisons based on the characteristics of the household or the Household Reference Person (HRP). A degree of caution is required in interpreting because the sampling errors at these levels can be high, especially where the sample size is small. The total sample size across the three years is given at the top of each column as an indication of the reliability of the figures. Due to the risk of sampling errors these comparisons have been averaged over the three years ended 31st March 2005. The possible relationships between household characteristics should also be considered when interpreting the figures e.g. there may be links between age of the household reference person, the composition of their household, their occupation and income.

2. Although the figures for the comparisons based on the characteristics of the household or the Household Reference Person are averages for a three year period, useful comparisons can still be made with the annual 2004-05 averages for the UK as a whole.

3. The purchases and expenditure tables contain data from both household food and drink and eating out. The energy and nutrient intake tables not only include the combined intakes from food brought into the home and eaten out but also the contributions from soft drinks, alcoholic drinks and confectionery.

4. For a more detailed breakdown of the data please refer to the datasets which are published on the Defra website at: http://statistics.defra.gov.uk/esg/publications/efs/datasets/default.asp

Income quintiles

5 Table 8.1 shows average purchased quantities and expenditure for the three years from April 2002 to March 2005 for both household and food and drink eaten out by income quintile, based on gross weekly household income.

6 Table 8.2 shows the average daily energy and nutrient intake from all food and drink by income quintile. The first income quintile contains the lowest income households. The fifth or highest income quintile contains the households with the highest income. There are 5 quintiles in all, each representing twenty per cent of the population of households. When interpreting the data, account should be taken of the average age of the Household Reference Person and average numbers of adults and children in the households.

7 Certain foods showed a marked variation in purchasing habits across the income quintiles 1 to 5. Household purchases of milk and cream, fats and oils, sugars and preserves, and cereals and beverages showed a clear decline across the income quintiles from quintile 1 (lowest income) to quintile 5 (highest income). Household purchases of cheese, fruit and alcoholic drinks showed the opposite trend. Expenditure on eating out increased across the quintiles, with households in the lowest income quintile spending £5.25 per person per week compared with £16.48 per person per week in households in the highest income quintile. Intakes of alcohol increased across the income quintiles culminating in an average of 14 grams per person per day in households in the highest income quintile.

First (lowest) income quintile households

8 For food and drink brought into the home, households in the first income quintile purchased the largest quantities of non-carcase meat and meat products and sugar and preserves but purchased the lowest amounts of cheese, carcase meat, vegetables (excluding fresh and processed potatoes), fruit, soft drinks and alcoholic drinks.

9 Members of these households also had the lowest purchases and expenditure of food and drink eaten outside the home with only 21 per cent of the total food and drink expenditure being spent on eating out, compared with 39 per cent in fifth (i.e. highest) income quintile households. First income quintile households spent 14 per cent less than the UK average on household food and drink but 47 per cent less on food and drink eaten out.

10 Household members in the first income quintile had the lowest intakes of alcohol but also the lowest intakes of vitamin C, the latter probably as a result of the low quantities of fruit purchased by these households. Intakes of niacin equivalent were also lowest in first income quintile households. In contrast, average intakes of vitamin B12 and vitamin A were highest in this quintile.

Second income quintile households

11 Purchases of all household food and beverage items, excepting cheese, sugar and preserves and fruit, were highest in second income quintile households. Members of these households spent 7.8 per cent less on household food and drink and 36 per cent less on food and drink eaten out than the UK average. 25 per cent of the total food and drink expenditure in second income quintile homes was spent on eating out compared to the UK average of 33 per cent. Households in the second income quintile had the highest average energy intake and the highest intakes of vitamin E and zinc.

Third income quintile households

12 Households in the third income quintile spent 7.4 per cent less than the UK average on household food and drink and 14 per cent less on eating out. However, spending on eating out represented 31 per cent of the total food and drink expenditure in these households, the closest equivalent to the UK average of 33 per cent. Daily per capita intakes of energy and many nutrients in third income quintile households was comparable with that in the UK as a whole.

Fourth income quintile households

13 Purchases for home consumption of fish, fresh and processed potatoes, and vegetables excluding potatoes were lowest in fourth income quintile households. Members of these households spent 2.8 per cent less on household food and drink and 7.1 per cent more on food and drink eaten out than the UK average. In fourth income quintile households, eating out expenditure represented 35 per cent of the total food and drink expenditure whereas for the UK as a whole the proportion was 33 per cent. Fourth income quintile household members had the lowest daily per capita intakes of energy, cholesterol and vitamin A.

Fifth (highest) income quintile households

14 Households in the fifth income quintile had the highest household purchases of cheese, fruit and alcoholic drinks and the lowest household purchases of milk and cream, sugar and preserves, fresh and processed potatoes and confectionery. Fifth income quintile households spent 14 per cent of the household food and drink budget on alcoholic drinks compared with the average for the UK of 12 per cent.

15 These households had the highest purchased quantities and expenditure on food and drink eaten outside the home with 39 per cent of the total food and drink expenditure being spent on eating out, compared to the UK average of 33 per cent. Fifth income quintile household food and drink expenditure was 12 per cent above the UK average. In contrast, expenditure on food and drink eaten out was 46 per cent higher.

16 Fifth income quintile households had the lowest energy intakes excluding energy from alcohol. As a probable result of the higher quantity of fruit purchases in these households, vitamin C and β-carotene intakes were highest in this quintile.

Table 8.1 Income quintile analysis of purchases and expenditure (average April 2002 to March 2005)

		Quintile 1	Quintile 2	Quintile 3	Quintile 4	Quintile 5
Number of households in sample		4 226	4 336	4 235	4 093	3 883
Average age of HRP		59	57	49	46	45
Average number of adults per household		1.2	1.6	1.9	2.2	2.4
Average number of children per household		0.3	0.4	0.6	0.7	0.7
Lower boundary (gross w'kly h'hold income (£))		0	205	375	579	885
Household purchases		*grams per person per week unless otherwise stated*				
Milk and cream	ml	2 280	2 203	2 034	1 895	1 803
Cheese		99	101	110	110	127
Carcase meat		218	254	224	224	223
Other meat and meat products		848	833	815	824	806
Fish		170	169	147	146	158
Eggs	no.	2.0	1.8	1.6	1.5	1.5
Fats and oils		228	225	189	167	155
Sugar and preserves		202	181	145	113	98
Fresh and processed potatoes		918	966	878	836	737
Vegetables excluding potatoes		1 065	1 131	1 062	1 061	1 141
Fruit		1 094	1 168	1 112	1 138	1 352
Total cereals		1 724	1 702	1 614	1 584	1 551
Beverages		72	68	55	49	49
Soft drinks (a)	ml	1 593	1 715	1 896	1 981	1 866
Alcoholic drinks	ml	544	648	736	826	894
Confectionery		125	139	130	130	123
Eating out purchases		*grams per person per week unless otherwise stated*				
Indian, Chinese and Thai meals or dishes		8	11	17	23	35
Meat and meat products		52	73	92	105	120
Fish and fish products		9	13	13	14	17
Cheese and egg dishes and pizza		13	17	23	29	35
Potatoes		53	68	84	91	98
Vegetables excluding potatoes		21	28	33	35	43
Sandwiches		29	44	64	87	118
Ice creams, desserts and cakes		18	24	29	33	38
Beverages	ml	89	115	139	159	175
Soft drinks including milk	ml	184	256	352	423	497
Alcoholic drinks	ml	400	499	628	751	831
Confectionery		12	18	21	23	24
Household expenditure		*pence per person per week*				
Milk and cream		159	157	151	147	153
Cheese		48	50	55	57	74
Carcase meat		99	117	107	106	117
Other meat and meat products		332	345	355	386	422
Fish		93	96	86	89	109
Eggs		21	18	17	16	18
Fats and oils		42	42	36	32	35
Sugar and preserves		22	20	16	14	14
Fresh and processed potatoes		95	102	103	105	98
Vegetables excluding potatoes		147	159	159	172	221
Fruit		142	154	149	150	202
Total cereals		332	350	352	374	411
Beverages		47	47	40	38	40
All other foods		100	108	111	121	141
Soft drinks		63	70	79	85	88
Alcoholic drinks		164	207	240	265	350
Confectionery		72	83	78	82	84
Total all food and drink excluding alcohol		1 814	1 918	1 895	1 975	2 227
Total all food and drink		1 979	2 125	2 135	2 240	2 577
Eating out expenditure		*pence per person per week*				
Total all food and drink excluding alcohol		346	483	641	794	1 129
Total alcoholic drinks		179	232	323	412	519
Total all food and drink		525	715	964	1 206	1 648

(a) Converted to unconcentrated equivalent by applying a factor of 5 to concentrated and low calorie concentrated soft drinks

Table 8.2 Income quintile analysis of intakes from all food and drink (average April 2002 to March 2005) (a)

		Quintile 1	Quintile 2	Quintile 3	Quintile 4	Quintile 5
Number of households in sample		4 226	4 336	4 235	4 093	3 883
Average age of HRP		59	57	49	46	45
Average number of adults per household		1.2	1.6	1.9	2.2	2.4
Average number of children per household		0.3	0.4	0.6	0.7	0.7
Lower boundary (gross w'kly h'hold income (£))		0	205	375	579	885
		\multicolumn{5}{c}{*intakes per person per day*}
Energy	kcal	2 270	2 337	2 256	2 237	2 245
	MJ	9.5	9.8	9.5	9.4	9.4
Energy excluding alcohol	kcal	2 219	2 273	2 182	2 154	2 150
Protein	g	76.3	78.2	75.8	76.3	77.5
Fat	g	94	96	92	90	90
Fatty acids:						
Saturates	g	37.1	37.8	35.9	35.1	35.4
Mono-unsaturates	g	33.9	34.9	33.4	32.9	32.8
Poly-unsaturates	g	16.4	17.0	16.3	16.1	15.9
Cholesterol	mg	271	267	254	250	257
Carbohydrate (b)	g	285	292	281	276	274
Total sugars	g	138	142	135	132	131
Non-milk extrinsic sugars	g	93	96	92	90	87
Starch	g	147	149	145	144	143
Fibre (c)	g	13.7	14.4	13.8	13.9	14.3
Alcohol	g	7	9	11	12	14
Calcium	mg	1 016	1 015	978	960	958
Iron	mg	11.6	12.0	11.7	11.9	12.1
Zinc	mg	9.1	9.3	9.0	9.0	9.1
Magnesium	mg	270	280	273	275	284
Sodium (d)	g	2.92	2.98	2.96	2.99	3.00
Potassium	g	3.02	3.15	3.04	3.04	3.11
Thiamin	mg	1.60	1.66	1.62	1.64	1.67
Riboflavin	mg	2.02	2.03	1.93	1.90	1.91
Niacin equivalent	mg	32.4	33.7	33.4	34.2	35.0
Vitamin B6	mg	2.3	2.4	2.3	2.4	2.4
Vitamin B12	µg	7.0	6.7	6.3	6.1	6.1
Folate	µg	276	287	277	278	288
Vitamin C	mg	64	68	68	70	78
Vitamin A:						
Retinol	µg	611	559	530	484	502
β-carotene	µg	1 842	1 960	1 884	1 901	2 034
Retinol equivalent	µg	926	893	851	806	845
Vitamin D	µg	3.50	3.44	3.24	3.18	3.12
Vitamin E	mg	12.16	12.66	12.18	12.01	11.81
		\multicolumn{5}{c}{*as a percentage of total food and drink energy excluding alcohol*}
Fat	%	38.1	38.1	37.8	37.7	37.8
Fatty acids:						
Saturates	%	15.1	15.0	14.8	14.7	14.8
Mono-unsaturates	%	13.8	13.8	13.8	13.7	13.8
Poly-unsaturates	%	6.6	6.7	6.7	6.7	6.6
Carbohydrate	%	48.2	48.1	48.3	48.1	47.7
Non-milk extrinsic sugars	%	15.8	15.9	15.8	15.6	15.2
Protein	%	13.8	13.8	13.9	14.2	14.4

continued

Table 8.2 continued

		Quintile 1	Quintile 2	Quintile 3	Quintile 4	Quintile 5
		\multicolumn{5}{c}{*as a percentage of weighted reference nutrient intake (e)*}
Energy (f)	%	95	97	96	95	95
Energy excluding alcohol (f)	%	93	94	93	92	91
Protein	%	146	149	152	154	154
Calcium	%	132	131	126	122	120
Iron	%	91	97	96	97	98
Zinc	%	105	105	103	102	102
Magnesium	%	92	95	94	94	95
Sodium (d)	%	178	181	185	187	184
Potassium	%	86	89	89	89	89
Thiamin	%	168	172	175	179	181
Riboflavin	%	148	150	150	149	149
Niacin equivalent	%	211	215	216	220	222
Vitamin B6	%	168	176	176	179	179
Vitamin B12	%	455	435	423	407	402
Folate	%	112	121	126	130	134
Vitamin C	%	137	149	154	161	180
Vitamin A (retinol equivalent)	%	128	124	122	116	121

(a) Contributions from pharmaceutical sources are not recorded by the survey
(b) Available carbohydrate, calculated as monosaccharide equivalent
(c) As non-starch polysaccharides
(d) (i) Excludes sodium from table salt (ii) The RNI for sodium is the amount that is sufficient for 97 per cent of the population. In May 2003 the Scientific Advisory Committee on Nutrition made recommendations about the maximum amount of salt that people should be eating, i.e. that the average salt intake for adults should be no more than 6 grams per day, equivalent to 2.4 grams of sodium per day
(e) Department of Health, 'Dietary Reference Values for Food Energy and Nutrients for the United Kingdom', HMSO 1991
(f) As a percentage of Estimated Average Requirement

Household composition

17 The size and composition of a household, together with the age of the HRP and average gross weekly household income, have a significant effect on food purchases, expenditure and energy and nutrient intakes.

18 Table 8.3 shows purchased quantities and expenditure per capita for both household and food and drink eaten out by household composition as averages for the three years ended 31st March 2005.

19 Table 8.4 shows the daily energy and nutrient intake per capita from all food and drink by household composition as averages for the three years ended 31st March 2005.

Adult only households

20 Household food and drink purchases and expenditure was highest in households with one, two or three adults and no children. On average, adult only households spent 7.2 per cent more than the UK average on food and drink eaten at home and 25 per cent more on eating out. Expenditure on food eaten at home remained highest in one adult households but when alcohol drinks were included, two adult households had the highest household expenditure. Households with 4 or more adults and no children had the highest spend on eating out which accounted for 45 per cent of the household's total food and drink expenditure and was 48 per cent higher than the UK average. As expected, households that contain only adults had the highest average daily intake of energy per person and, as a consequence, higher intakes of all nutrients.

Households with children

21 Households with children continued to have the lowest levels of purchases in all foods, with the exception of soft drinks which was highest in single parent households. On average, households with children spent 25 per cent less than the UK average on food and drink eaten at home and 31 per cent less on eating out. The lowest levels of food and drink spending were in households with 2 adults and 4 or more children, where household expenditure was 36 per cent less and eating out expenditure 53 per cent less than the UK average.

22 Households with 3 or more children had the lowest energy intake per person which reflects the lower energy requirements of children. In addition, these households had the lowest intakes of many nutrients.

Table 8.3 Household composition analysis of purchases and expenditure (average April 2002 to March 2005)

No. of adults:		1	1	2	2	2	2	2	3 or more	3 or more	3 or more	4 or more
No. of children:		0	1 or more	0	1	2	3	4 or more	0	1 or 2	3 or more	0
Number of households in sample		5 677	1 365	6 913	1 531	1 999	633	209	1 150	771	101	421
Average age of HRP		59	35	56	39	39	39	39	54	47	43	49
Average gross weekly household income (£)		283	289	590	746	792	778	950	823	898	923	1 010
Household purchases		*grams per person per week unless otherwise stated*										
Milk and cream	ml	2 477	1 731	2 204	1 954	1 802	1 694	1 656	2 005	1 730	1 749	1 677
Cheese		123	82	136	108	100	78	73	124	95	66	102
Carcase meat		221	142	301	192	169	155	154	288	234	155	224
Other meat and meat products		962	714	912	783	717	657	653	899	795	586	757
Fish		223	94	208	121	108	114	89	165	117	99	132
Eggs	no.	2.1	1.2	2.0	1.4	1.2	1.1	1.2	1.8	1.4	1.1	1.6
Fats and oils		238	137	232	146	130	128	148	205	169	200	188
Sugar and preserves		207	100	179	96	88	86	118	153	113	109	120
Fresh and processed potatoes		877	730	999	784	712	694	698	950	812	747	837
Vegetables excluding potatoes		1 292	737	1 424	978	834	697	688	1 227	932	693	1 036
Fruit		1 590	708	1 528	1 012	953	807	712	1 254	968	696	1 002
Total cereals		1 885	1 384	1 777	1 511	1 463	1 367	1 438	1 682	1 537	1 373	1 556
Beverages		87	36	76	43	35	29	31	64	40	38	48
Soft drinks (a)	ml	1 487	2 210	1 562	2 009	2 098	2 099	2 063	1 860	2 056	1 754	1 890
Alcoholic drinks	ml	837	347	969	793	661	500	357	925	543	467	790
Confectionery		139	119	139	125	133	130	122	119	119	113	91
Eating out purchases		*grams per person per week unless otherwise stated*										
Indian, Chinese and Thai meals or dishes		23	11	24	20	15	15	15	31	19	18	30
Meat and meat products		89	81	88	100	93	89	77	99	123	95	125
Fish and fish products		17	7	19	12	10	8	8	16	13	7	12
Cheese and egg dishes and pizza		22	24	22	27	29	27	26	26	31	22	32
Potatoes		82	77	82	83	84	80	82	81	93	81	91
Vegetables excluding potatoes		46	19	43	31	25	19	17	40	28	18	35
Sandwiches		74	51	78	86	66	52	43	97	88	52	112
Ice creams, desserts and cakes		28	27	32	29	33	31	37	30	27	26	23
Beverages	ml	190	53	189	136	109	79	46	171	110	65	156
Soft drinks including milk	ml	231	410	271	421	411	435	406	400	566	458	566
Alcoholic drinks	ml	865	162	793	502	354	244	161	1 113	784	243	1 346
Confectionery		8	39	10	22	30	36	43	14	32	38	19
Household expenditure		*pence per person per week*										
Milk and cream		193	120	171	155	143	123	113	150	123	117	125
Cheese		66	40	74	57	53	39	35	64	47	32	49
Carcase meat		117	57	153	90	79	67	62	140	100	63	109
Other meat and meat products		440	286	425	372	337	282	263	416	347	235	354
Fish		136	47	136	75	66	52	41	104	66	45	78
Eggs		25	12	23	15	13	11	11	20	14	10	16
Fats and oils		52	22	49	30	24	22	21	40	27	26	34
Sugar and preserves		26	10	22	11	10	9	13	18	11	9	13
Fresh and processed potatoes		99	102	104	104	99	92	94	104	104	89	100
Vegetables excluding potatoes		219	108	232	167	138	106	94	192	141	94	157
Fruit		229	89	220	139	125	101	82	167	119	83	133
Total cereals		416	310	401	374	353	308	297	382	348	282	352
Beverages		64	24	57	32	27	21	19	48	28	25	35
All other foods		136	91	141	123	107	89	82	120	106	74	110
Soft drinks		69	88	72	89	85	82	79	81	89	69	87
Alcoholic drinks		312	108	368	247	204	149	97	304	155	148	230
Confectionery		87	73	88	79	83	78	72	74	73	67	58
Total all food and drink excluding alcohol		2 374	1 479	2 367	1 913	1 742	1 483	1 378	2 121	1 745	1 318	1 811
Total all food and drink		2 686	1 587	2 735	2 160	1 946	1 633	1 475	2 424	1 900	1 466	2 042
Eating out expenditure		*pence per person per week*										
Total all food and drink excluding alcohol		758	452	873	733	655	544	441	861	749	513	886
Total alcoholic drinks		445	105	447	282	195	129	86	591	407	151	781
Total all food and drink		1 203	557	1 320	1 014	850	672	527	1 452	1 156	664	1 667

(a) Converted to unconcentrated equivalent by applying a factor of 5 to concentrated and low calorie concentrated soft drinks

Table 8.4 Household composition analysis of intakes from all food and drink (average April 2002 to March 2005) (a)

	No. of adults:		1		2				3 or more			4 or more
	No. of children:		0	1 or more	0	1	2	3	4 or more	0	1 or 2	3 or more	0
Number of households in sample			5 677	1 365	6 913	1 531	1 999	633	209	1 150	771	101	421
Average age of HRP			59	35	56	39	39	39	39	54	47	43	49
Average gross weekly household income (£)			283	289	590	746	792	778	950	823	898	923	1 010
			intakes per person per day										
Energy		kcal	2 582	1 894	2 550	2 122	2 005	1 869	1 936	2 423	2 190	1 902	2 217
		MJ	10.9	8.0	10.7	8.9	8.4	7.9	8.1	10.2	9.2	8.0	9.3
Energy excluding alcohol		kcal	2 487	1 865	2 447	2 054	1 951	1 831	1 909	2 317	2 126	1 864	2 117
Protein		g	88.7	61.4	88.7	71.7	66.3	60.6	60.2	83.7	72.8	58.5	74.8
Fat		g	105	78	104	86	81	75	79	97	89	80	88
Fatty acids:													
Saturates		g	41.7	30.3	40.7	33.8	32.0	29.8	30.7	37.8	33.8	28.8	32.8
Mono-unsaturates		g	37.6	28.4	37.6	31.2	29.2	27.4	28.8	35.6	32.6	29.3	32.0
Poly-unsaturates		g	18.0	13.8	18.2	14.9	13.9	13.1	14.2	17.3	16.5	16.7	16.8
Cholesterol		mg	312	198	304	234	212	195	196	284	238	192	242
Carbohydrate (b)		g	318	245	309	266	256	243	256	295	276	243	275
Total sugars		g	156	117	149	125	123	116	120	139	128	114	125
Non-milk extrinsic sugars		g	101	85	97	85	86	82	88	93	90	81	87
Starch		g	162	128	160	140	133	127	135	155	148	129	150
Fibre (c)		g	20.7	11.1	20.4	15.1	13.4	11.6	11.2	20.6	16.5	11.3	20.7
Alcohol		g	9	4	11	8	6	5	4	10	6	5	7
Calcium		mg	1 152	823	1 099	925	875	803	795	1 029	902	778	917
Iron		mg	13.8	9.4	13.7	11.2	10.6	9.6	9.7	12.5	11.0	9.4	11.3
Zinc		mg	10.5	7.2	10.5	8.5	7.8	7.2	7.1	9.8	8.6	7.1	8.8
Magnesium		mg	330.7	213.0	325.1	258.7	238.9	215.0	210.0	301.5	255.4	209.9	271.7
Sodium (d)		g	3.41	2.52	3.34	2.83	2.67	2.40	2.36	3.18	2.76	2.18	2.86
Potassium		g	3.65	2.42	3.65	2.89	2.65	2.40	2.36	3.37	2.85	2.36	2.99
Thiamin		mg	1.89	1.33	1.90	1.55	1.47	1.34	1.36	1.75	1.54	1.29	1.58
Riboflavin		mg	2.34	1.55	2.25	1.80	1.70	1.56	1.54	2.05	1.75	1.56	1.78
Niacin equivalent		mg	38.5	26.8	39.1	31.7	29.5	26.9	26.6	37.4	32.4	25.6	33.6
Vitamin B6		mg	2.7	1.9	2.8	2.2	2.1	2.0	2.0	2.7	2.3	1.9	2.4
Vitamin B12		µg	7.9	5.0	7.5	5.6	5.2	5.0	4.7	6.7	5.7	5.1	5.6
Folate		µg	338	212	340	259	242	218	216	312	258	215	278
Vitamin C		mg	84	54	84	68	62	55	51	75	65	52	66
Vitamin A:													
Retinol		µg	710	353	677	455	388	340	330	560	443	488	418
β-carotene		µg	2 261	1 406	2 363	1 776	1 624	1 389	1 398	2 157	1 659	1 254	1 774
Retinol equivalent		µg	1 096	590	1 079	756	663	575	565	926	723	701	719
Vitamin D		µg	4.06	2.46	3.87	3.11	2.66	2.50	2.41	3.44	2.78	2.61	2.96
Vitamin E		mg	13.41	10.45	13.41	11.41	10.53	9.98	10.69	12.73	12.17	12.51	12.44
			as a percentage of total food and drink energy excluding alcohol										
Fat		%	37.4	37.5	37.7	37.3	37.0	37.0	37.2	37.2	37.2	38.5	36.4
Fatty acids:													
Saturates		%	14.9	14.6	14.8	14.7	14.7	14.6	14.5	14.5	14.1	13.8	13.6
Mono-unsaturates		%	13.4	13.7	13.7	13.6	13.4	13.4	13.6	13.6	13.6	14.1	13.3
Poly-unsaturates		%	6.4	6.7	6.6	6.5	6.4	6.4	6.7	6.6	6.9	8.0	7.0
Carbohydrate		%	47.4	49.3	46.9	48.1	49.0	49.6	50.2	46.9	48.1	48.7	47.6
Non-milk extrinsic sugars		%	15.0	17.0	14.7	15.3	16.4	16.7	17.2	14.9	15.8	16.3	15.0
Protein		%	14.1	13.2	14.3	13.9	13.5	13.2	12.6	14.2	13.5	12.5	13.8

continued

Table 8.4 continued

	No. of Adults:		1		2					3 or more			4 or more
	No. of Children:		0	1 or more	0	1	2	3	4 or more	0	1 or 2	3 or more	0
									as a percentage of weighted reference nutrient intake (e)				
Energy (f)		%	109	90	106	94	90	85	88	99	90	82	89
Energy excluding alcohol (f)		%	105	89	102	91	88	83	87	94	87	80	85
Protein		%	160	150	160	150	149	142	145	150	138	124	133
Calcium		%	148	111	141	124	119	109	107	131	110	97	116
Iron		%	132	76	125	93	90	83	85	110	87	76	94
Zinc		%	117	89	114	100	91	84	83	106	95	81	94
Magnesium		%	105	84	103	94	90	83	82	95	83	74	85
Sodium (d)		%	192	172	188	183	178	163	162	179	162	137	161
Potassium		%	94	82	94	88	86	81	82	87	78	71	77
Thiamin		%	196	157	197	172	166	153	156	178	159	140	158
Riboflavin		%	177	137	168	148	143	133	132	153	135	126	132
Niacin equivalent		%	247	192	245	211	200	184	184	229	200	167	202
Vitamin B6		%	189	159	192	173	168	159	161	183	164	145	165
Vitamin B12		%	473	379	448	390	382	379	364	403	359	352	334
Folate		%	152	114	152	131	127	116	117	140	120	106	125
Vitamin C		%	189	138	189	162	155	140	132	169	151	126	148
Vitamin A (retinol equivalent)		%	153	95	149	113	102	90	89	128	103	105	99

(a) Contributions from pharmaceutical sources are not recorded by the survey
(b) Available carbohydrate, calculated as monosaccharide equivalent
(c) As non-starch polysaccharides
(d) (i) Excludes sodium from table salt (ii) The RNI for sodium is the amount that is sufficient for 97 per cent of the population. In May 2003 the Scientific Advisory Committee on Nutrition made recommendations about the maximum amount of salt that people should be eating, i.e. that the average salt intake for adults should be no more than 6 grams per day, equivalent to 2.4 grams of sodium per day
(e) As a percentage of Estimated Average Requirement

Age group of Household Reference Person

23 From 2001-02 the concept of Household Reference Person (HRP) was adopted on all government-sponsored surveys replacing the concept of head of household. The HRP is the person who:

- owns the household accommodation, or
- is legally responsible for the rent of the accommodation, or
- has the household accommodation by virtue of their employment or personal relationship to the owner who is not a member of the household.

If more than one person meet these criteria the HRP will be the one with the higher income. If the incomes are the same then the eldest is chosen.

24 The age of the HRP is often related to the composition of the household and, to a lesser extent, its income group and level of eating out. In particular it is necessary to consider the average number of children per household before interpreting the results. For example, there are practically no children in households where the HRP is aged between 65 and 74, leading to higher average energy intakes per person than in households with children. The survey results by the HRP age group should therefore be interpreted with caution: for example, purchases of soft drinks were highest in the 65 to 74 group, which could be due to visits by grandchildren.

25 Table 8.5 shows the purchased quantities and expenditure for both household and food and drink eaten out by HRP age group as averages for the three years ended 31st March 2005.

26 Table 8.6 shows the daily energy and nutrient intake from all food and drink by HRP age group as averages for the three years ended 31st March 2005.

Household and eating out

27 As expected, household purchases of most food items rose steadily with the age of the HRP to a peak in the 65 and under 75 age group. The exceptions were sugar and beverages which continued to rise with age, soft drinks which peaked with the "40 and under 50" age group, and cheese and non-carcase meat which peaked with households where the HRP was aged 50 and under 65. The purchases of food and drink items for consumption outside the home showed more variation across the age groups but overall purchases of most food and drink items eaten out was lowest in the "75 and over" age group.

Household reference person aged less than thirty

28 Purchased quantities of all household food items were lowest in households where the HRP was aged under 30. For food items eaten outside the home, households in this group and the group where the HRP was aged between 40 and under 50 purchased the most ethnic meals, meat and meat products, sandwiches and soft drinks.

29 The per capita spend in households where the HRP was aged less than 30 was £17.84 on food and drink for home consumption which was 26 per cent less than the UK average for all households. In these households, 11 per cent of the household expenditure was spent on alcoholic drinks for home consumption.

30. Members of households with a HRP aged less than thirty had the highest spend on food and drink eaten out at £13.57 per person per week, which represented 43 per cent of their total expenditure on all food and drink, and was 21 per cent above the UK average.

31. Intakes of energy and all nutrients are lowest in the "under 30" age group but the percentage of energy (excluding alcohol) derived from carbohydrate is highest.

Household reference person aged between thirty and under forty

32. Households where the HRP is aged 30 and under 40 spent £19.46 per person per week on food and drink for home consumption which was 19 per cent lower than the UK average. Expenditure on food and drink eaten out was 6.9 per cent lower than for all UK households and as a percentage of total food and drink spending was 35 per cent, compared with the UK average of 32 per cent.

Household reference person aged between forty and under fifty

33. Compared with other HRP age groups, the households where the HRP was between 40 and 50 tended to have the highest numbers of children in the household. These households purchased the most soft drinks for home consumption. When eating out they purchased the most cheese and egg dishes and pizza, chips, cakes and ice creams and confectionery, which might indicate a pattern of eating out driven by the preferences of the children. Weekly per capita spending on eating out at £10.48 was 35 per cent of the total food and drink budget.

Household reference person aged between fifty and under sixty-five

34. Purchased quantities of and expenditure on alcoholic drinks brought into the home was highest in households where the HRP was aged 50 and under 65. These households purchased the highest quantities of fish, vegetables, beverages and alcoholic drinks eaten out. Combined food and drink expenditure was £39.43, of which £12.76 was spent on eating out. This represented 32 per cent of the total. The weekly per capita household expenditure at £26.67 on all food and drink was 11 per cent higher than the UK average.

Household reference person aged between sixty-five and under seventy-five

35. Purchased quantities for home consumption of most food items, apart from non-carcase meat, sugar, beverages and soft drinks, was highest in households where the HRP is aged 65 and under 75. Members of households in this HRP age group had the highest weekly per capita expenditure on food and drink brought into the home at £26.49, which was 10 per cent more than the average for all UK households. Expenditure on eating out, at £8.32, was 24 per cent of the total spend on food and drink.

36. Intakes of energy and the intakes of most nutrients were highest in this HRP age group.

Household reference person aged seventy-five and over

37. Members of households in the aged "75 and over" group were the highest purchasers of sugar and beverages and the lowest purchasers of soft and alcoholic drinks.

38. Expenditure on household food and drink, at £23.50, was similar to the UK average for all households whereas expenditure on food and drink eaten out at £5.18 was 53 per cent below the UK average and represented only 19 per cent of the total expenditure on all food and drink.

Table 8.5 Age of Household Reference Person analysis of purchases and expenditure (average April 2002 to March 2005)

		under 30	30 and under 40	40 and under 50	50 and under 65	65 and under 75	75 and over
Number of households in sample		1 952	4 134	4 185	5 187	2 898	2 417
Average number of adults per household		1.7	1.8	2.2	2.0	1.7	1.4
Average number of children per household		0.7	1.2	0.9	0.1	0.0	0.0
Average gross weekly household income (£)		493	669	753	616	336	254
Household purchases		\multicolumn{6}{l}{grams per person per week unless otherwise stated}
Milk and cream	ml	1 541	1 759	1 835	2 220	2 589	2 475
Cheese		92	98	107	136	125	90
Carcase meat		125	161	212	302	331	265
Other meat and meat products		647	712	850	950	916	782
Fish		103	115	133	194	231	222
Eggs	no.	1.2	1.2	1.4	2.0	2.2	2.0
Fats and oils		116	134	164	227	282	264
Sugar and preserves		77	88	111	172	227	251
Fresh and processed potatoes		618	686	822	1 035	1 097	886
Vegetables excluding potatoes		739	860	993	1 397	1 486	1 196
Fruit		784	917	1 039	1 471	1 689	1 557
Total cereals		1 317	1 446	1 578	1 786	1 934	1 775
Beverages		30	36	46	74	90	93
Soft drinks (a)	ml	1 921	1 921	2 120	1 814	1 469	1 077
Alcoholic drinks	ml	702	717	781	927	669	479
Confectionery		92	116	137	135	154	142
Eating out purchases		\multicolumn{6}{l}{grams per person per week unless otherwise stated}
Indian, Chinese and Thai meals or dishes		25	22	25	22	11	6
Meat and meat products		113	99	113	90	60	43
Fish and fish products		11	12	13	17	17	14
Cheese and egg dishes and pizza		31	28	33	23	13	7
Potatoes		87	85	94	81	68	54
Vegetables excluding potatoes		33	30	33	39	36	31
Sandwiches		104	80	89	80	35	18
Ice creams, desserts and cakes		26	31	34	31	28	21
Beverages	ml	107	129	140	180	156	116
Soft drinks including milk	ml	492	425	489	324	139	66
Alcoholic drinks	ml	903	513	673	856	555	284
Confectionery		22	27	32	14	4	2
Household expenditure		\multicolumn{6}{l}{pence per person per week}
Milk and cream		114	137	137	170	197	191
Cheese		46	52	56	72	68	54
Carcase meat		55	72	98	152	167	142
Other meat and meat products		320	336	387	429	390	348
Fish		58	66	79	123	146	141
Eggs		13	13	15	22	26	24
Fats and oils		21	25	30	46	60	56
Sugar and preserves		8	10	12	21	28	32
Fresh and processed potatoes		94	96	105	110	102	80
Vegetables excluding potatoes		132	151	163	221	211	175
Fruit		98	124	139	208	237	218
Total cereals		346	349	371	393	392	362
Beverages		23	27	34	57	64	62
All other foods		110	110	117	134	126	114
Soft drinks		82	82	90	82	63	47
Alcoholic drinks		204	223	247	342	276	218
Confectionery		58	73	86	85	95	85
Total all food and drink excluding alcohol		1 580	1 723	1 921	2 326	2 373	2 132
Total all food and drink		1 784	1 946	2 167	2 667	2 649	2 350
Eating out expenditure		\multicolumn{6}{l}{pence per person per week}
Total all food and drink excluding alcohol		812	738	805	820	579	404
Total alcoholic drinks		545	310	361	456	253	132
Total all food and drink		1 357	1 048	1 166	1 276	832	536

(a) Converted to unconcentrated equivalent by applying a factor of 5 to concentrated and low calorie concentrated soft drinks

Table 8.6 Age of Household Reference Person analysis of intakes from all food and drink (average April 2002 to March 2005) (a)

		under 30	30 and under 40	40 and under 50	50 and under 65	65 and under 75	75 and over
Number of households in sample		1 952	4 134	4 185	5 187	2 898	2 417
Average number of adults per household		1.7	1.8	2.2	2.0	1.7	1.4
Average number of children per household		0.7	1.2	0.9	0.1	0.0	0.0
Average gross weekly household income (£)		493	669	753	616	336	254
		\multicolumn{6}{c}{*intakes per person per day*}
Energy	kcal	1 835	1 978	2 238	2 563	2 663	2 371
	MJ	7.7	8.4	9.5	10.9	11.3	9.9
Energy excluding alcohol	kcal	1 759	1 916	2 164	2 462	2 583	2 315
Protein	g	61.0	66.1	75.4	89.2	91.4	79.0
Fat	g	72	80	91	105	110	98
Fatty acids:							
Saturates	g	27.6	31.0	35.4	40.7	44.3	40.2
Mono-unsaturates	g	26.5	29.0	33.2	38.0	39.7	35.1
Poly-unsaturates	g	13.3	14.3	16.3	18.5	18.7	16.1
Cholesterol	mg	193	213	248	305	325	288
Carbohydrate (b)	g	230	249	278	311	327	297
Total sugars	g	107	116	133	150	163	155
Non-milk extrinsic sugars	g	75	80	93	99	105	101
Starch	g	123	133	145	161	164	142
Fibre (c)	g	10.8	12.0	13.4	16.4	17.3	15.2
Alcohol	g	11	9	11	14	11	8
Calcium	mg	798	859	949	1 107	1 171	1 057
Iron	mg	9.4	10.4	11.6	13.6	14.2	12.6
Zinc	mg	7.2	7.8	8.8	10.5	10.9	9.5
Magnesium	mg	220	238	269	324	332	290
Sodium (d)	g	2.54	2.64	2.98	3.41	3.46	4.09
Potassium	g	2.40	2.61	2.96	3.64	3.84	4.16
Thiamin	mg	1.32	1.44	1.60	1.87	1.95	1.71
Riboflavin	mg	1.50	1.67	1.86	2.23	2.43	2.21
Niacin equivalent	mg	27.6	29.4	33.7	39.4	39.3	33.0
Vitamin B6	mg	1.9	2.1	2.3	2.7	2.8	2.3
Vitamin B12	µg	4.7	5.2	6.0	7.4	8.1	7.3
Folate	µg	218	238	269	331	350	308
Vitamin C	mg	58	61	66	82	86	74
Vitamin A:							
Retinol	µg	341	397	461	652	759	714
β-carotene	µg	1 364	1 571	1 844	2 360	2 497	2 093
Retinol equivalent	µg	571	663	773	1 053	1 186	1 073
Vitamin D	µg	2.54	2.74	2.99	3.80	4.26	3.82
Vitamin E	mg	10.23	10.82	12.11	13.65	13.72	11.91
		\multicolumn{6}{c}{*as a percentage of total food and drink energy excluding alcohol*}
Fat	%	37.1	37.4	37.9	38.2	38.4	38.2
Fatty acids:							
Saturates	%	14.1	14.6	14.7	14.9	15.4	15.6
Mono-unsaturates	%	13.6	13.6	13.8	13.9	13.8	13.6
Poly-unsaturates	%	6.8	6.7	6.8	6.8	6.5	6.2
Carbohydrate	%	49.1	48.8	48.2	47.3	47.5	48.2
Non-milk extrinsic sugars	%	16.1	15.6	16.0	15.1	15.3	16.3
Protein	%	13.9	13.8	13.9	14.5	14.1	13.7

continued

Table 8.6 continued

		under 30	30 and under 40	40 and under 50	50 and under 65	65 and under 75	75 and over
		\multicolumn{6}{l}{as a percentage of weighted reference nutrient intake (e)}
Energy (f)	%	81	88	93	107	114	103
Energy excluding alcohol (f)	%	78	85	90	103	111	101
Protein	%	128	145	149	163	166	145
Calcium	%	111	118	119	140	151	136
Iron	%	78	89	91	125	144	129
Zinc	%	85	92	98	115	120	107
Magnesium	%	81	89	90	103	106	93
Sodium (d)	%	165	174	178	193	195	230
Potassium	%	73	83	84	95	99	107
Thiamin	%	145	161	168	196	207	182
Riboflavin	%	124	139	146	169	184	169
Niacin equivalent	%	183	197	211	249	255	219
Vitamin B6	%	146	161	171	191	194	165
Vitamin B12	%	327	373	392	453	491	436
Folate	%	111	123	128	150	158	138
Vitamin C	%	138	149	157	186	194	167
Vitamin A (retinol equivalent)	%	86	101	112	147	166	151

(a) Contributions from pharmaceutical sources are not recorded by the survey
(b) Available carbohydrate, calculated as monosaccharide equivalent
(c) As non-starch polysaccharides
(d) (i) Excludes sodium from table salt (ii) The RNI for sodium is the amount that is sufficient for 97 per cent of the population. In May 2003 the Scientific Advisory Committee on Nutrition made recommendations about the maximum amount of salt that people should be eating, i.e. that the average salt intake for adults should be no more than 6 grams per day, equivalent to 2.4 grams of sodium per day
(e) Department of Health, 'Dietary Reference Values for Food Energy and Nutrients for the United Kingdom', HMSO 1991
(f) As a percentage of Estimated Average Requirement

Age at which Household Reference Person ceased full-time education

39 The age at which the HRP ceased full-time education is related to the age of the HRP, the composition of the household and, given that graduates tend to earn more than non-graduates, the household income. It should be noted that in households in the "aged 14 and under" group there are fewer adults and children and the average age of the HRP is much older. These factors, and how they apply to each particular age group, should be taken into account when interpreting the results.

40 Table 8.7 shows averages for the three years ended 31st March 2005 of purchases and expenditure for both household and food and drink eaten out by HRP education age group.

41 Table 8.8 shows the averages for the three years ended 31st March 2005 of daily energy and nutrient intake from all food and drink by HRP education age group.

Household

42 Household purchases of most types of food apart from cheese, vegetables (excluding fresh and processed potatoes), fruit and alcoholic drinks tend to be highest in households where the HRP ceased full time education aged 15 or under. For cheese, vegetables (excluding fresh and processed potatoes), fruit and alcoholic drinks is was households where the HRP ceased full-time education aged 22 or over that purchased the highest quantities. These households purchased the least carcase meat, other meat and meat products, sugar and preserves, fresh and processed potatoes, cereals and confectionery.

43 Households in the "aged 16" group spent the least per person per week on food and drink brought into the home. At £20.71 this was 10 per cent below the UK average. The highest expenditure on household food and drink was in households in the "aged 22 or over" group where the average weekly per capita spend was 9.4 per cent more than the average for all UK households.

Eating out

44 The quantity of food and drink eaten out tended to be highest in households where the HRP ceased full-time education aged 17 or older and lowest in households where the HRP ceased full-time education aged 14 or under. Households in the "aged 15" group purchased the most alcoholic drinks for consumption outside the home.

45 Households in the "aged 14 and under" group spent £5.53 per person per week on food and drink for consumption outside the home which was 51 per cent lower than the UK average. The highest expenditure on food and drink for consumption outside the home was in households in the "aged 22 or over" group where the average weekly per capita spend of £14.85 was 32 per cent more than the average for all UK households.

Intakes

46 The percentage of food energy derived from saturated fatty acids was highest in households where the HRP ceased full-time education aged 14 or under. This percentage decreased as the age at which the HRP left education increased and was lowest when the HRP left full-time education aged 22 and over. Average energy intake and the intakes of fat, carbohydrate and sodium were lowest in households where the HRP ceased full-time education aged 22 and over.

The intake of vitamin C was highest in this group. Intakes of most vitamins and minerals were lowest in the "aged 16" group. The percentage of energy (excluding alcohol) derived from fat was highest and from carbohydrate was lowest in households where the HRP ceased full-time education aged 15.

Table 8.7 Age at which Household Reference Person ceased full-time education analysis of purchases and expenditure (average April 2002 to March 2005)

		Aged 14 & under	Aged 15	Aged 16	Aged 17 & under 19	Aged 19 & under 22	Aged 22 & over
Number of households in sample		2 618	4 168	6 351	3 544	2 028	1 970
Average age of HRP		74	58	46	46	45	44
Average number of adults per household		1.5	1.9	1.9	1.9	1.9	1.9
Average number of children per household		0.1	0.3	0.8	0.7	0.6	0.6
Average gross weekly household income (£)		244	407	535	633	811	1 021
Household purchases		\multicolumn{6}{c}{grams per person per week unless otherwise stated}
Milk and cream	ml	2 478	2 216	1 900	1 912	1 837	1 956
Cheese		97	119	102	113	126	128
Carcase meat		292	291	207	210	208	191
Other meat and meat products		861	970	842	784	717	659
Fish		203	170	130	155	168	177
Eggs	no.	2.1	1.9	1.4	1.5	1.5	1.6
Fats and oils		271	233	160	176	169	160
Sugar and preserves		243	179	118	122	114	107
Fresh and processed potatoes		1 007	1 110	859	777	652	593
Vegetables excluding potatoes		1 197	1 227	946	1 071	1 166	1 290
Fruit		1 335	1 147	949	1 234	1 497	1 594
Total cereals		1 854	1 770	1 543	1 585	1 587	1 542
Beverages		89	72	49	51	49	49
Soft drinks (a)	ml	1 332	1 925	2 092	1 884	1 615	1 492
Alcoholic drinks	ml	505	812	758	796	781	852
Confectionery		141	147	133	125	119	97
Eating out purchases		\multicolumn{6}{c}{grams per person per week unless otherwise stated}
Indian, Chinese and Thai meals or dishes		6	17	19	24	31	34
Meat and meat products		49	85	103	104	100	91
Fish and fish products		13	13	12	14	17	18
Cheese and egg dishes and pizza		9	21	27	28	29	32
Potatoes		56	75	90	87	88	83
Vegetables excluding potatoes		27	33	31	36	41	41
Sandwiches		22	60	74	86	101	108
Ice creams, desserts and cakes		20	25	29	33	38	37
Beverages	ml	110	152	140	145	150	156
Soft drinks including milk	ml	118	306	423	403	407	406
Alcoholic drinks	ml	409	792	654	691	615	594
Confectionery		6	17	26	22	21	19
Household expenditure		\multicolumn{6}{c}{pence per person per week}
Milk and cream		177	160	141	153	151	162
Cheese		49	58	51	61	73	77
Carcase meat		145	139	94	103	110	100
Other meat and meat products		353	405	378	377	369	345
Fish		121	100	77	94	108	120
Eggs		23	19	15	17	19	20
Fats and oils		53	44	30	34	38	37
Sugar and preserves		27	18	13	16	17	17
Fresh and processed potatoes		92	115	110	97	86	79
Vegetables excluding potatoes		159	169	148	183	218	249
Fruit		177	152	124	170	216	237
Total cereals		356	370	356	378	395	393
Beverages		57	51	36	39	41	41
All other foods		109	114	108	126	141	143
Soft drinks		56	80	86	82	78	75
Alcoholic drinks		185	253	225	281	324	352
Confectionery		80	88	80	80	81	72
Total all food and drink excluding alcohol		2 036	2 080	1 846	2 009	2 141	2 168
Total all food and drink		2 221	2 334	2 071	2 289	2 465	2 521
Eating out expenditure		\multicolumn{6}{c}{pence per person per week}
Total all food and drink excluding alcohol		379	595	685	828	999	1 073
Total alcoholic drinks		174	375	342	403	404	413
Total all food and drink		553	969	1 026	1 231	1 403	1 485

(a) Converted to unconcentrated equivalent by applying a factor of 5 to concentrated and low calorie concentrated soft drinks

Table 8.8 Age at which Household Reference Person ceased full-time education analysis of intakes from all food and drink (average April 2002 to March 2005) (a)

		Aged 14 & under	Aged 15	Aged 16	Aged 17 & under 19	Aged 19 & under 22	Aged 22 & over
Number of households in sample		2 618	4 168	6 351	3 544	2 028	1 970
Average age of HRP		74	58	46	46	45	44
Average number of adults per household		1.5	1.9	1.9	1.9	1.9	1.9
Average number of children per household		0.1	0.3	0.8	0.7	0.6	0.6
Average gross weekly household income (£)		244	407	535	633	811	1 021
		intakes per person per day					
Energy	kcal	2 468	2 511	2 185	2 237	2 207	2 159
	MJ	10.4	10.6	9.2	9.4	9.3	9.1
Energy excluding alcohol	kcal	2 412	2 427	2 112	2 155	2 125	2 074
Protein	g	83	86	74	75	75	75
Fat	g	102	103	88	90	88	85
Fatty acids:							
Saturates	g	40.8	40.5	34.7	35.0	34.2	33.0
Mono-unsaturates	g	36.7	37.7	32.2	32.7	32.0	30.7
Poly-unsaturates	g	17.3	18.2	15.4	16.4	15.7	15.3
Cholesterol	mg	296	293	244	249	246	241
Carbohydrate (b)	g	311	307	273	278	276	270
Total sugars	g	154	148	130	132	129	126
Non-milk extrinsic sugars	g	103	100	91	89	85	79
Starch	g	156	159	142	146	146	144
Fibre (c)	g	15.3	15.4	13.1	14.0	14.4	15.0
Alcohol	g	8	12	10	12	12	12
Calcium	mg	1 084	1 081	940	955	940	953
Iron	mg	12.7	13.0	11.3	11.9	11.9	12.1
Zinc	mg	9.9	10.1	8.7	8.9	8.8	8.8
Magnesium	mg	294	305	262	277	279	287
Sodium (d)	g	3.04	3.34	2.94	2.92	2.81	2.72
Potassium	g	3.35	3.46	2.95	3.05	3.06	3.12
Thiamin	mg	1.77	1.80	1.57	1.64	1.64	1.65
Riboflavin	mg	2.23	2.17	1.84	1.90	1.86	1.89
Niacin equivalent	mg	34.9	37.8	32.8	33.6	33.2	33.0
Vitamin B6	mg	2.5	2.7	2.3	2.4	2.3	2.3
Vitamin B12	µg	7.4	7.2	5.9	6.1	5.9	6.0
Folate	µg	315	316	265	283	284	292
Vitamin C	mg	72	71	64	73	82	85
Vitamin A:							
Retinol	µg	657	639	471	502	497	491
β-carotene	µg	2 069	2 155	1 743	1 917	1 994	2 077
Retinol equivalent	µg	1 012	1 007	766	826	835	842
Vitamin D	µg	3.84	3.78	3.02	3.13	3.16	3.08
Vitamin E	mg	12.67	13.50	11.59	12.17	11.69	11.47
		as a percentage of total food and drink energy excluding alcohol					
Fat	%	38.0	38.4	37.6	37.7	37.3	36.9
Fatty acids:							
Saturates	%	15.2	15.0	14.8	14.6	14.5	14.3
Mono-unsaturates	%	13.7	14.0	13.7	13.7	13.6	13.3
Poly-unsaturates	%	6.5	6.7	6.6	6.8	6.7	6.7
Carbohydrate	%	48.3	47.5	48.4	48.3	48.6	48.8
Non-milk extrinsic sugars	%	16.0	15.5	16.1	15.5	14.9	14.3
Protein	%	13.7	14.1	14.0	14.0	14.1	14.4

continued

Table 8.8 continued

		Aged 14 & under	Aged 15	Aged 16	Aged 17 & under 19	Aged 19 & under 22	Aged 22 & over
		as a percentage of weighted reference nutrient intake (e)					
Energy (f)	%	107	107	94	96	94	92
Energy excluding alcohol (f)	%	104	103	91	93	91	89
Protein	%	153	161	150	151	149	148
Calcium	%	139	138	123	125	123	126
Iron	%	127	118	96	102	101	104
Zinc	%	110	113	98	101	100	100
Magnesium	%	95	100	91	95	95	98
Sodium (d)	%	173	193	181	179	171	166
Potassium	%	87	93	86	88	87	89
Thiamin	%	189	191	170	177	176	177
Riboflavin	%	170	167	147	152	147	150
Niacin equivalent	%	228	242	213	218	214	212
Vitamin B6	%	179	193	174	177	171	171
Vitamin B12	%	448	451	397	405	389	396
Folate	%	143	146	129	137	137	141
Vitamin C	%	162	164	152	173	194	199
Vitamin A (retinol equivalent)	%	142	143	112	121	121	122

(a) Contributions from pharmaceutical sources are not recorded by the survey
(b) Available carbohydrate, calculated as monosaccharide equivalent
(c) As non-starch polysaccharides
(d) (i) Excludes sodium from table salt (ii) The RNI for sodium is the amount that is sufficient for 97 per cent of the population. In May 2003 the Scientific Advisory Committee on Nutrition made recommendations about the maximum amount of salt that people should be eating, i.e. that the average salt intake for adults should be no more than 6 grams per day, equivalent to 2.4 grams of sodium per day
(e) Department of Health, 'Dietary Reference Values for Food Energy and Nutrients for the United Kingdom', HMSO 1991
(f) As a percentage of Estimated Average Requirement

Ethnic origin of Household Reference Person

47 Comparisons based on the ethnic origin of the household reference person show that patterns in certain household food and drink purchases and in eating out can be linked to the ethnic origin of the HRP. However, when interpreting the results it should be noted that 95 per cent of the sample were white HRP households.

48 Table 8.9 shows averages of purchases and expenditure for both household and food and drink eaten out by ethnic origin of the HRP for the three years ended 31st March 2005.

49 Table 8.10 shows the averages for daily energy and nutrient intakes from all food and drink by ethnic origin of the HRP for the three years ended 31st March 2005.

Household

50 For household food and drink, "White HRP" households purchased the highest quantities of milk and cream, cheese, meat products, fresh and processed potatoes, beverages, soft drinks, alcoholic drinks and confectionery. "Asian HRP" households purchased the most vegetables (excluding fresh and processed potatoes), cereals and fats and purchases of fish were highest in "Black HRP" households. Members of "Mixed HRP" households had the highest purchased quantities of carcase meat, eggs, sugar and preserves and fruit.

51 Household food and drink expenditure was highest in "White HRP" households where £24.26 was the average spend. This was 5.3 per cent more than the UK average for all households. In comparison, "Asian HRP" households spent £15.04 per person per week which was 35 per cent less than the UK average.

Eating out

52 When eating out "Chinese and other HRP" households purchased the highest quantities of Indian, Chinese or Thai meals, fish and fish products and cheese, egg and pizza dishes. For all other types of food and drink purchased for consumption outside the home it was "White HRP" households which purchased the highest quantities.

53 Both "Chinese and other HRP" and "White HRP" households spent similar amounts on food and non-alcoholic drinks for consumption outside the home but "White HRP" households had the highest expenditure when alcohol purchases were taken into account. "Asian HRP" households spent the least amount (£5.49) on eating out. This was 51 per cent less than the average for all UK households.

Intakes

54 Households classified as "White" had the highest daily per capita intakes of energy and most nutrients. In addition these households had the highest percentages of energy (excluding alcohol) derived from total fat and saturated fatty acids and protein. "Chinese and other HRP" households had the lowest intakes of energy and many vitamins and minerals in addition to having the lowest percentage of energy (excluding alcohol) derived from fat.

Table 8.9 Ethnic origin of Household Reference Person analysis of purchases and expenditure (average April 2002 to March 2005)

		Asian/ Asian British	Black/ Black British	Chinese and others	Mixed	White
Number of households in sample		420	368	88	96	18 710
Average age of HRP		43	44	43	41	52
Average number of adults per household		2.4	1.7	2.1	1.7	1.8
Average number of children per household		1.1	0.9	0.7	0.8	0.5
Average gross weekly household income (£)		640	424	584	362	565
Household purchases		\multicolumn{5}{l}{grams per person per week unless otherwise stated}
Milk and cream	ml	1 948	1 319	1 098	1 580	2 031
Cheese		48	44	71	90	117
Carcase meat		185	210	226	239	229
Other meat and meat products		420	709	667	721	844
Fish		124	211	125	134	158
Eggs	no.	1.6	1.8	1.9	2.0	1.6
Fats and oils		275	203	150	186	182
Sugar and preserves		134	141	98	191	138
Fresh and processed potatoes		460	485	406	576	875
Vegetables excluding potatoes		1 132	1 022	1 132	1 095	1 099
Fruit		1 197	1 243	1 089	1 351	1 200
Total cereals		1 756	1 485	1 528	1 486	1 620
Beverages		28	34	37	50	58
Soft drinks (a)	ml	1 474	1 822	1 207	1 689	1 860
Alcoholic drinks	ml	229	288	181	534	808
Confectionery		70	61	82	102	135
Eating out purchases		\multicolumn{5}{l}{grams per person per week unless otherwise stated}
Indian, Chinese and Thai meals or dishes		23	14	68	15	21
Meat and meat products		57	81	91	80	96
Fish and fish products		13	9	24	9	14
Cheese and egg dishes and pizza		26	15	29	22	26
Potatoes		60	61	80	60	84
Vegetables excluding potatoes		23	19	23	33	35
Sandwiches		57	43	68	44	78
Ice creams, desserts and cakes		19	22	30	21	31
Beverages	ml	72	61	105	102	149
Soft drinks including milk	ml	297	295	363	299	372
Alcoholic drinks	ml	108	219	173	432	688
Confectionery		20	19	15	13	21
Household expenditure		\multicolumn{5}{l}{pence per person per week}
Milk and cream		126	93	87	112	156
Cheese		23	22	36	45	62
Carcase meat		74	78	96	86	112
Other meat and meat products		163	243	248	274	389
Fish		60	93	80	77	98
Eggs		16	17	21	20	18
Fats and oils		35	29	20	31	37
Sugar and preserves		14	15	13	19	17
Fresh and processed potatoes		68	62	57	72	103
Vegetables excluding potatoes		159	208	243	238	283
Fruit		155	145	143	170	166
Total cereals		313	276	285	333	376
Beverages		18	20	33	30	44
All other foods		83	93	82	104	123
Soft drinks		75	88	59	71	80
Alcoholic drinks		82	93	96	153	278
Confectionery		40	39	45	67	84
Total all food and drink excluding alcohol		1 423	1 520	1 549	1 751	2 149
Total all food and drink		1 504	1 613	1 645	1 903	2 426
Eating out expenditure		\multicolumn{5}{l}{pence per person per week}
Total all food and drink excluding alcohol		478	429	804	546	765
Total alcoholic drinks		70	138	109	218	378
Total all food and drink		549	567	913	764	1 143

(a) Converted to unconcentrated equivalent by applying a factor of 5 to concentrated and low calorie concentrated soft drinks

Table 8.10 Ethnic origin of Household Reference Person analysis of intakes from all food and drink (average April 2002 to March 2005) (a)

		Asian/ Asian British	Black/ Black British	Chinese and others	Mixed	White
Number of households in sample		420	368	88	96	18 710
Average age of HRP		43	44	43	41	52
Average number of adults per household		2.4	1.7	2.1	1.7	1.8
Average number of children per household		1.1	0.9	0.7	0.8	0.5
Average gross weekly household income (£)		640	424	584	362	565
		\multicolumn{5}{c}{intakes per person per day}
Energy	kcal	2 132	1 930	1 909	2 063	2 295
	MJ	9.0	8.1	8.0	8.7	9.6
Energy excluding alcohol	kcal	2 113	1 902	1 887	2 015	2 213
Protein	g	62.3	63.6	66.2	67.9	78.2
Fat	g	85	76	74	84	93
Fatty acids:						
Saturates	g	28.0	24.7	25.2	30.6	36.8
Mono-unsaturates	g	31.2	28.6	27.7	30.9	33.7
Poly-unsaturates	g	20.4	17.2	15.9	16.6	16.1
Cholesterol	mg	194	218	224	243	262
Carbohydrate (b)	g	292	257	255	264	284
Total sugars	g	111	113	97	131	137
Non-milk extrinsic sugars	g	71	79	64	92	93
Starch	g	181	144	158	133	146
Fibre (c)	g	13.1	11.9	12.2	12.4	14.3
Alcohol	g	3	4	3	7	12
Calcium	mg	819	665	652	823	1 000
Iron	mg	9.8	10.2	9.5	10.3	12.1
Zinc	mg	7.5	7.6	8.0	7.9	9.2
Magnesium	mg	226	226	225	243	284
Sodium (d)	g	1.73	1.96	1.98	2.43	3.07
Potassium	g	2.48	2.42	2.44	2.71	3.17
Thiamin	mg	1.34	1.35	1.30	1.42	1.68
Riboflavin	mg	1.52	1.50	1.34	1.65	1.99
Niacin equivalent	mg	25.1	28.8	28.0	30.2	34.6
Vitamin B6	mg	1.9	2.0	1.9	2.1	2.5
Vitamin B12	µg	4.8	5.4	4.6	5.3	6.4
Folate	µg	228	240	224	252	291
Vitamin C	mg	63	71	60	73	72
Vitamin A:						
Retinol	µg	353	356	335	367	543
β-carotene	µg	1 503	1 387	1 670	1 561	1 979
Retinol equivalent	µg	605	591	615	630	879
Vitamin D	µg	2.08	3.17	2.16	2.89	3.33
Vitamin E	mg	14.67	12.40	10.92	12.43	12.02
		\multicolumn{5}{c}{as a percentage of total food and drink energy excluding alcohol}
Fat	%	36.3	35.9	35.3	37.4	37.8
Fatty acids:						
Saturates	%	11.9	11.7	12.0	13.7	15.0
Mono-unsaturates	%	13.3	13.5	13.2	13.8	13.7
Poly-unsaturates	%	8.7	8.1	7.6	7.4	6.5
Carbohydrate	%	51.9	50.7	50.7	49.1	48.0
Non-milk extrinsic sugars	%	12.7	15.6	12.7	17.1	15.7
Protein	%	11.8	13.4	14.0	13.5	14.1

continued

Table 8.10 continued

		Asian/ Asian British	Black/ Black British	Chinese and others	Mixed	White
		as a percentage of weighted reference nutrient intake (e)				
Energy (f)	%	93	85	80	91	98
Energy excluding alcohol (f)	%	92	84	79	89	95
Protein	%	129	134	129	143	154
Calcium	%	109	89	84	113	130
Iron	%	84	87	79	90	106
Zinc	%	86	89	89	92	104
Magnesium	%	80	81	75	88	96
Sodium (d)	%	109	124	118	156	184
Potassium	%	74	73	68	83	89
Thiamin	%	146	149	136	157	180
Riboflavin	%	123	123	104	136	156
Niacin equivalent	%	165	191	177	200	224
Vitamin B6	%	144	153	137	158	180
Vitamin B12	%	330	372	298	366	418
Folate	%	113	120	106	128	139
Vitamin C	%	151	172	141	175	170
Vitamin A (retinol equivalent)	%	90	88	88	94	127

(a) Contributions from pharmaceutical sources are not recorded by the survey
(b) Available carbohydrate, calculated as monosaccharide equivalent
(c) As non-starch polysaccharides
(d) (i) Excludes sodium from table salt (ii) The RNI for sodium is the amount that is sufficient for 97 per cent of the population. In May 2003 the Scientific Advisory Committee on Nutrition made recommendations about the maximum amount of salt that people should be eating, i.e. that the average salt intake for adults should be no more than 6 grams per day, equivalent to 2.4 grams of sodium per day
(e) Department of Health, 'Dietary Reference Values for Food Energy and Nutrients for the United Kingdom', HMSO 1991
(f) As a percentage of Estimated Average Requirement

Socio-economic classification of Household Reference Person

55 Unlike most other comparisons in this chapter, the socio-economic classification of the HRP bears little relation to the age of the HRP and the household composition. However, the socio-economic classification of the HRP is strongly related to the average gross weekly household income and this should not be overlooked when interpreting the results.

56 Table 8.11 shows averages of purchases and expenditure for both household and food and drink eaten out by the socio-economic classification of the HRP for the three years ended 31st March 2005.

57 Table 8.12 shows the averages for daily energy and nutrient intakes from all food and drink by the socio-economic classification of the HRP for the three years ended 31st March 2005.

Household

58 The households where the HRP was in the "Higher professional" category purchased the largest quantities of cheese, vegetables (excluding fresh and processed potatoes), fruit and alcoholic drinks whereas the households where the HRP was in the "Never worked and long-term unemployed" category had the lowest purchases of most food items apart from eggs, fats and oils, sugar and preserves, fresh and processed potatoes and soft drinks. Purchases of vegetables in the households where the HRP was in the "Never worked & long-term unemployed" category were considerably lower than in the all other categories where the HRP was employed in some capacity.

59 Weekly expenditure on household food and drink was highest at £26.41 per person in households where the HRP was in the category "Large employer, higher managerial". This was 15 per cent more than the UK average for all households. The lowest per capita expenditure was in households where the HRP was in the category "Never worked and long-term unemployed" and at £15.54 was 33 per cent lower than the UK average.

Eating out

60 Purchased quantities of most food items eaten out were highest in households where the HRP was in the "Large employer, higher managerial" or in the "Higher professional" categories. Purchases of alcoholic drinks were highest in households where the HRP was classified as "Lower supervisory" whereas the highest weekly per capita expenditure on alcoholic drinks for consumption outside the home, at £4.88, was in households where the HRP was in the "Large employer, higher managerial" category. Households where the HRP was in the "Never worked and long-term unemployed" category purchased the lowest quantities of food items eaten out.

61 The lowest weekly expenditure per person on food and drink for consumption outside the home (£8.49) was in households where the HRP was in the "Never worked and long-term unemployed" category. This represented 35 per cent of their total food and drink expenditure and was slightly above the UK average for all households of 33 per cent. The highest weekly expenditure on food and drink for consumption outside the home was in households where the HRP was in the "Large employer, higher managerial" category where the average weekly spend per person was £17.31. This was 54 per cent higher than the UK average and represented 40 per cent of the total food and drink budget in those households.

Intakes

62 Average intakes of energy and most nutrients were lowest in households where the HRP was in the "Never worked and long-term unemployed" category. Energy, protein, fat and carbohydrate and sodium intakes were highest in households where the HRP was in the "Lower supervisory" category. The highest intakes of a number of vitamins and minerals were found mostly in households where the HRP was classified as "Higher professional".

Table 8.11 Socio-economic classification of Household Reference Person analysis of purchases and expenditure (average April 2002 to March 2005)

		Large employer, higher managerial & professional	Small employer & own account worker	Higher professional	Intermediate	Lower professional, managerial, higher technical & supervisory	Lower supervisory & technical occupations	Never worked & long term unemployed	Routine	Semi-routine
Number of households in sample		917	1 274	1 336	1 308	3 800	1 502	400	1 597	1 718
Average age of HRP		44	47	43	42	43	43	39	45	43
Average number of adults per household		2.1	2.1	2.0	1.8	2.0	2.1	1.8	2.0	1.9
Average number of children per household		0.8	0.8	0.7	0.6	0.7	0.7	0.9	0.7	0.7
Average gross weekly household income (£)		1 299	630	1 096	561	803	607	231	460	454
Household purchases									*grams per person per week unless otherwise stated*	
Milk and cream	ml	1 831	1 973	1 888	1 826	1 828	1 841	1 661	1 927	1 970
Cheese		123	113	133	111	121	111	82	97	97
Carcase meat		221	251	202	184	214	222	175	222	200
Other meat and meat products		797	822	735	783	799	893	728	869	852
Fish		151	159	164	147	148	136	107	132	126
Eggs	no.	1.4	1.5	1.5	1.4	1.5	1.5	1.7	1.5	1.5
Fats and oils		142	183	149	153	157	173	205	183	179
Sugar and preserves		86	129	103	113	97	117	135	144	128
Fresh and processed potatoes		693	873	670	773	742	917	715	992	906
Vegetables excluding potatoes		1 127	1 063	1 194	1 006	1 116	1 007	774	966	939
Fruit		1 400	1 069	1 528	1 068	1 278	911	723	844	885
Total cereals		1 529	1 585	1 558	1 532	1 550	1 634	1 456	1 595	1 620
Beverages		47	51	49	47	50	48	38	49	49
Soft drinks (a)	ml	1 863	1 816	1 660	1 881	1 900	2 237	1 898	2 034	2 130
Alcoholic drinks	ml	907	760	919	741	882	891	514	745	696
Confectionery		129	122	107	121	128	138	100	130	131
Eating out purchases									*grams per person per week unless otherwise stated*	
Indian, Chinese and Thai meals or dishes		38	20	33	24	29	23	16	16	18
Meat and meat products		115	104	106	98	110	118	83	98	100
Fish and fish products		21	12	18	12	15	12	7	12	11
Cheese and egg dishes and pizza		33	28	35	28	30	30	29	27	26
Potatoes		100	86	96	84	92	94	61	82	86
Vegetables excluding potatoes		43	32	43	34	39	33	17	28	29
Sandwiches		119	74	128	94	103	81	54	65	70
Ice creams, desserts and cakes		44	30	40	33	35	28	22	26	25
Beverages	ml	187	108	175	142	151	179	68	143	153
Soft drinks including milk	ml	481	390	464	423	446	452	421	411	420
Alcoholic drinks	ml	717	755	736	729	726	803	540	776	650
Confectionery		23	24	21	27	23	24	23	28	26

continued

Table 8.11 continued

	Large employer, higher managerial & professional	Small employer & own account worker	Higher professional	Intermediate	Lower professional, managerial, higher technical & supervisory	Lower supervisory & technical occupations	Never worked & long term unemployed	Routine	Semi-routine
Household expenditure								*pence per person per week*	
Milk and cream	161	150	161	138	149	138	111	134	138
Cheese	73	61	80	57	67	53	39	45	47
Carcase meat	121	120	108	86	108	99	67	98	88
Other meat and meat products	429	389	399	360	399	391	274	361	354
Fish	110	96	112	84	98	76	52	68	65
Eggs	18	17	19	15	17	15	16	14	14
Fats and oils	35	36	35	29	33	30	29	30	31
Sugar and preserves	13	16	17	13	14	12	14	13	12
Fresh and processed potatoes	94	106	91	99	98	116	91	113	110
Vegetables excluding potatoes	228	175	237	169	203	146	106	131	133
Fruit	215	147	228	143	181	114	89	104	109
Total cereals	409	373	413	367	391	373	288	333	350
Beverages	40	39	41	36	40	35	25	34	34
All other foods	151	122	146	117	134	109	80	100	99
Soft drinks	84	80	81	83	87	90	81	84	86
Alcoholic drinks	371	252	378	245	322	244	133	189	184
Confectionery	89	77	76	76	85	83	59	77	76
Total all food and drink excluding alcohol	2 270	2 004	2 243	1 872	2 103	1 880	1 420	1 741	1 746
Total all food and drink	2 641	2 255	2 621	2 117	2 425	2 123	1 553	1 930	1 930
Eating out expenditure								*pence per person per week*	
Total all food and drink excluding alcohol	1 243	755	1 135	754	954	693	511	575	583
Total alcoholic drinks	488	408	464	407	449	400	339	349	333
Total all food and drink	1 731	1 163	1 599	1 161	1 403	1 093	849	924	916

(a) Converted to unconcentrated equivalent by applying a factor of 5 to concentrated and low calorie concentrated soft drinks

Table 8.12 Socio-economic classification of Household Reference Person analysis of intakes from all food and drink (average April 2002 to March 2005) (a)

		Large employer, higher managerial & professional	Small employer & own account worker	Higher professional	Intermediate	Lower professional, managerial, higher technical & supervisory	Lower supervisory & technical occupations	Never worked & long term unemployed	Routine	Semi-routine
Number of households in sample		917	1 274	1 336	1 308	3 800	1 502	400	1 597	1 718
Average age of HRP		44	47	43	42	43	43	39	45	43
Average number of adults per household		2.1	2.1	2.0	1.8	2.0	2.1	1.8	2.0	1.9
Average number of children per household		0.8	0.8	0.7	0.6	0.7	0.7	0.9	0.7	0.7
Average gross weekly household income (£)		1 299	630	1 096	561	803	607	231	460	454
									intakes per person per day	
Energy	kcal	2 217	2 262	2 224	2 147	2 212	2 312	1 987	2 258	2 246
	MJ	9.3	9.5	9.4	9.0	9.3	9.7	8.3	9.5	9.4
Energy excluding alcohol	kcal	2 123	2 183	2 130	2 069	2 123	2 228	1 936	2 187	2 180
Protein	g	77.1	77.3	76.5	72.5	76.1	78.2	63.9	75.3	74.5
Fat	g	88	93	88	85	89	94	83	92	91
Fatty acids:										
Saturates	g	34.9	36.5	34.7	33.1	34.5	36.3	30.3	35.2	35.2
Mono-unsaturates	g	32.0	33.7	31.7	31.0	32.2	34.4	30.6	33.6	33.3
Poly-unsaturates	g	15.4	16.3	15.3	15.3	15.7	16.9	16.2	16.8	16.4
Cholesterol	mg	251	260	249	234	249	256	221	249	244
Carbohydrate (b)	g	272	277	276	270	272	285	250	283	283
Total sugars	g	130	131	131	128	129	134	114	133	132
Non-milk extrinsic sugars	g	85	89	84	87	86	93	82	93	93
Starch	g	142	146	145	142	143	152	135	150	151
Fibre (c)	g	14.3	13.7	14.8	13.3	14.2	13.9	10.9	13.4	13.2
Alcohol	g	13	11	13	11	13	12	7	10	9
Calcium	mg	952	970	969	930	950	974	825	956	959
Iron	mg	12.2	11.7	12.3	11.3	12.0	11.8	9.5	11.4	11.3
Zinc	mg	9.0	9.1	9.0	8.5	8.9	9.2	7.5	8.9	8.8
Magnesium	mg	285	273	289	263	280	278	219	266	264
Sodium (d)	g	2.98	2.95	2.92	2.88	2.98	3.12	2.45	3.00	2.93
Potassium	g	3.13	3.06	3.17	2.92	3.08	3.09	2.47	3.00	2.97
Thiamin	mg	1.69	1.64	1.69	1.58	1.66	1.63	1.30	1.60	1.57
Riboflavin	mg	1.91	1.92	1.92	1.82	1.89	1.88	1.55	1.87	1.86
Niacin equivalent	mg	34.9	34.3	34.3	32.5	34.2	34.8	27.8	33.3	32.9
Vitamin B6	mg	2.4	2.4	2.4	2.3	2.4	2.5	1.9	2.4	2.4
Vitamin B12	µg	6.0	6.3	6.0	5.8	6.0	6.1	5.4	6.2	6.0
Folate	µg	291	282	295	269	285	275	219	271	266
Vitamin C	mg	81	69	85	67	75	64	53	60	62

continued

Table 8.12 continued

		Large employer, higher managerial & professional	Small employer & own account worker	Higher professional	Intermediate	Lower professional, managerial, higher technical & supervisory	Lower supervisory & technical occupations	Never worked & long term unemployed	Routine	Semi-routine
Vitamin A:										
Retinol	µg	490	513	497	472	484	489	395	488	465
β-carotene	µg	2 061	1 868	2 062	1 847	1 991	1 841	1 275	1 749	1 702
Retinol equivalent	µg	838	829	845	785	821	803	611	785	754
Vitamin D	µg	3.05	3.26	3.16	3.05	3.11	3.26	2.65	3.16	3.03
Vitamin E	mg	11.38	12.07	11.46	11.51	11.77	12.60	12.00	12.60	12.33

as a percentage of total food and drink energy excluding alcohol

Fat	%	37.5	38.3	37.1	37.1	37.5	37.9	38.4	37.8	37.6
Fatty acids:										
Saturates	%	14.8	15.1	14.7	14.4	14.6	14.7	14.1	14.5	14.5
Mono-unsaturates	%	13.6	13.9	13.4	13.5	13.7	13.9	14.2	13.8	13.8
Poly-unsaturates	%	6.5	6.7	6.4	6.7	6.7	6.8	7.5	6.9	6.8
Carbohydrate	%	48.0	47.6	48.6	48.9	48.1	48.0	48.4	48.5	48.7
Non-milk extrinsic sugars	%	15.1	15.3	14.9	15.7	15.2	15.7	15.9	16.0	15.9
Protein	%	14.5	14.2	14.4	14.0	14.3	14.0	13.2	13.8	13.7

as a percentage of weighted reference nutrient intake (e)

Energy (f)	%	95	96	95	93	94	98	86	96	97
Energy excluding alcohol (f)	%	91	93	91	89	91	94	83	93	94
Protein	%	154	153	152	145	151	155	132	150	150
Calcium	%	124	126	127	122	124	127	108	124	125
Iron	%	103	101	105	95	100	100	79	98	96
Zinc	%	101	101	101	97	101	103	86	100	100
Magnesium	%	98	93	99	91	96	95	77	91	91
Sodium (d)	%	183	179	178	176	180	190	153	183	180
Potassium	%	90	87	91	84	88	88	73	86	86
Thiamin	%	181	175	180	170	178	173	141	171	169
Riboflavin	%	152	151	152	145	150	148	125	148	148
Niacin equivalent	%	224	219	220	211	220	222	180	214	213
Vitamin B6	%	181	178	178	172	178	180	146	178	176
Vitamin B12	%	401	413	399	381	392	404	364	408	397
Folate	%	141	136	143	130	137	133	107	130	129
Vitamin C	%	192	162	199	158	177	151	127	142	147
Vitamin A (retinol equivalent)	%	122	120	122	115	119	116	90	114	110

(a) Contributions from pharmaceutical sources are not recorded by the survey
(b) Available carbohydrate, calculated as monosaccharide equivalent
(c) As non-starch polysaccharides
(d) (i) Excludes sodium from table salt (ii) The RNI for sodium is the amount that is sufficient for 97 per cent of the population. In May 2003 the Scientific Advisory Committee on Nutrition made recommendations about the maximum amount of salt that people should be eating, i.e. that the average salt intake for adults should be no more than 6 grams per day, equivalent to 2.4 grams of sodium per day
(e) Department of Health, 'Dietary Reference Values for Food Energy and Nutrients for the United Kingdom', HMSO 1991
(f) As a percentage of Estimated Average Requirement

Economic activity of Household Reference Person

63 The economic status of the HRP is generally related to the age of the HRP, the household income and the household composition. The data shown in this analysis should be interpreted with some caution given that in households where the HRP is retired there are practically no children. In addition, the sample size for households where the HRP is on a Government Training Scheme is small which has a bearing on the precision of the estimates.

64 Table 8.13 shows the averages of purchases and expenditure for both food and drink purchased for the household and for consumption outside the home by economic activity of HRP for the three years ended 31st March 2005.

65 Table 8.14 shows the averages of daily energy and nutrient intake from all food and drink by economic activity of HRP for the three years ended 31st March 2005.

Household

66 Household purchases of most food items was highest in households where the HRP was retired, but purchases of cheese, eggs, fats and oils, fresh and processed potatoes and soft drinks were highest in households where the HRP was attending a Government Training Scheme. It was households where the HRP was a full-time employee that purchased the most alcoholic drinks but the least eggs, fats and oils, and fresh and processed potatoes.

67 The highest expenditure on food and drink brought home at £25.17 per person per week was in households where the HRP was retired, which represented 78 per cent of their total weekly expenditure on all food and drink and was 9.2 per cent higher than the UK average for all households.

68 Households where the HRP was attending a Government Training Scheme had the lowest per capita weekly expenditure on household food and drink at £15.33, which represented 73 per cent of their total weekly expenditure and was 33 per cent lower than the UK average.

Eating out

69 Households where the HRP was a full-time employee were the highest purchasers of all food and drink for consumption outside the home apart from fish and fish products and confectionery. The weekly per person eating out expenditure in these households was £13.39 which was 37 per cent of their total weekly expenditure on all food and drink and was 19 per cent higher than the UK average for all households.

70 Households where the HRP was either retired or on a Government Training Scheme had the lowest purchases of food and drink for consumption outside the home. The households where the HRP was on a Government Training Scheme spent the least on food and drink for consumption outside the home at £5.59 per person per week. This was 27 per cent of their total food and drink expenditure and was about half the UK average. However, households where the HRP was retired spent the lowest proportion of their total expenditure on food and drink purchased for consumption outside the home.

Intakes

71 Households where the HRP was retired had the highest energy intake and the highest intakes of almost all nutrients. This could reflect the absence of children in most of these households. The lowest intakes of energy and most nutrients were found in households where the HRP was unemployed.

72 The highest percentages of energy (excluding alcohol) derived from fat and the lowest percentages of energy (excluding alcohol) derived from carbohydrate and protein were found in households where the HRP was on a Government Training Scheme. Households where the HRP was a part-time employee had the highest percentage of energy (excluding alcohol) derived from carbohydrate and the lowest from fats whereas households where the HRP was self employed had the highest percentage derived from protein.

Table 8.13 Economic activity of Household Reference Person analysis of purchases and expenditure (average April 2002 to March 2005)

		Economically active					Economically inactive	
		Full time employees	Part time employees	Self employed	Un- employed	Gov't Training Scheme	Retired	Other
Number of households in sample		9 080	1 628	1 629	394	17	5 310	2 713
Average age of HRP		42	46	47	40	39	74	45
Average number of adults per household		2.1	1.8	2.1	1.7	1.4	1.5	1.7
Average number of children per household		0.7	0.8	0.8	0.8	0.7	0.0	0.8
Average gross weekly household income (£)		803	475	772	233	139	283	275
Household purchases		\multicolumn{7}{l}{grams per person per week unless otherwise stated}
Milk and cream	ml	1 838	1 906	1 962	1 819	1 800	2 551	2 035
Cheese		114	108	120	89	133	114	97
Carcase meat		208	203	244	216	183	304	215
Other meat and meat products		821	789	805	789	855	864	807
Fish		140	140	170	129	107	226	132
Eggs	no.	1.4	1.6	1.5	1.8	2.4	2.2	1.8
Fats and oils		156	169	180	203	306	274	198
Sugar and preserves		105	121	125	137	69	238	161
Fresh and processed potatoes		794	845	832	831	1 116	1 004	898
Vegetables excluding potatoes		1 036	1 050	1 133	945	710	1 361	1 002
Fruit		1 136	1 085	1 227	755	816	1 632	923
Total cereals		1 569	1 573	1 582	1 550	1 653	1 872	1 551
Beverages		48	49	53	44	24	92	53
Soft drinks (a)	ml	2 005	1 899	1 736	1 753	2 923	1 321	1 917
Alcoholic drinks	ml	849	661	830	756	310	588	651
Confectionery		130	121	119	100	136	151	115
Eating out purchases		\multicolumn{7}{l}{grams per person per week unless otherwise stated}
Indian, Chinese and Thai meals or dishes		27	20	24	16	6	9	10
Meat and meat products		115	85	101	68	68	52	71
Fish and fish products		15	13	13	7	3	16	10
Cheese and egg dishes and pizza		32	25	29	24	9	10	18
Potatoes		95	81	86	60	58	62	65
Vegetables excluding potatoes		38	30	34	20	7	33	23
Sandwiches		102	70	80	44	57	27	43
Ice creams, desserts and cakes		34	30	32	23	6	25	22
Beverages	ml	170	119	120	77	77	137	87
Soft drinks including milk	ml	464	399	393	334	328	107	308
Alcoholic drinks	ml	778	575	752	440	692	439	506
Confectionery		25	26	23	29	18	4	22
Household expenditure		\multicolumn{7}{l}{pence per person per week}
Milk and cream		145	143	155	121	122	195	137
Cheese		61	55	68	44	51	61	47
Carcase meat		101	92	122	87	51	156	93
Other meat and meat products		395	343	397	284	254	372	323
Fish		87	80	109	57	52	143	72
Eggs		16	16	17	18	20	25	18
Fats and oils		31	32	38	30	38	58	33
Sugar and preserves		13	14	17	14	7	29	16
Fresh and processed potatoes		103	102	102	96	134	93	102
Vegetables excluding potatoes		179	165	198	125	90	194	141
Fruit		156	145	177	93	80	227	121
Total cereals		383	351	389	301	273	378	318
Beverages		37	37	42	30	14	64	37
All other foods		125	112	131	85	102	121	97
Soft drinks		88	82	79	65	110	57	77
Alcoholic drinks		283	216	305	179	71	253	188
Confectionery		83	75	79	57	65	91	68
Total all food and drink excluding alcohol		2 002	1 842	2 119	1 507	1 462	2 264	1 700
Total all food and drink		2 285	2 058	2 424	1 686	1 533	2 517	1 888
Eating out expenditure		\multicolumn{7}{l}{pence per person per week}
Total all food and drink excluding alcohol		894	661	859	427	268	491	485
Total alcoholic drinks		445	320	422	227	291	199	253
Total all food and drink		1 339	981	1 281	654	559	690	738

(a) Converted to unconcentrated equivalent by applying a factor of 5 to concentrated and low calorie concentrated soft drinks

Table 8.14 Economic activity of Household Reference Person analysis of intakes from all food and drink (average April 2002 to March 2005) (a)

		Economically active					Economically inactive	
		Full time employees	Part time employees	Self employed	Un-employed	Gov't Training Scheme	Retired	Other
Number of households in sample		9 080	1 628	1 629	394	17	5 310	2 713
Average age of HRP		42	46	47	40	39	74	45
Average number of adults per household		2.1	1.8	2.1	1.7	1.4	1.5	1.7
Average number of children per household		0.7	0.8	0.8	0.8	0.7	0.0	0.8
Average gross weekly household income (£)		803	475	772	233	139	283	275
		intakes per person per day						
Energy	kcal	2 228	2 184	2 267	2 116	2 425	2 557	2 171
	MJ	9.4	9.2	9.5	8.9	10.2	10.7	9.1
Energy excluding alcohol	kcal	2 143	2 117	2 181	2 058	2 383	2 487	2 111
Protein	g	75.9	73.4	77.7	69.2	73.0	86.6	72.4
Fat	g	89	88	92	89	115	105	89
Fatty acids:								
Saturates	g	34.7	34.2	36.2	33.5	41.4	42.6	34.1
Mono-unsaturates	g	32.5	31.8	33.5	33.0	41.9	37.7	32.5
Poly-unsaturates	g	15.9	15.7	16.3	16.8	24.0	17.5	16.4
Cholesterol	mg	247	241	260	239	251	309	245
Carbohydrate (b)	g	276	276	277	260	282	319	272
Total sugars	g	131	130	131	117	121	160	129
Non-milk extrinsic sugars	g	89	88	88	82	85	104	89
Starch	g	146	146	146	143	161	158	143
Fibre (c)	g	13.8	13.6	14.2	12.1	13.5	16.6	13.0
Alcohol	g	12	10	12	8	6	10	9
Calcium	mg	954	942	973	883	989	1 126	941
Iron	mg	11.8	11.4	11.9	10.4	11.4	13.6	11.0
Zinc	mg	8.9	8.7	9.1	8.3	9.2	10.3	8.6
Magnesium	mg	276	265	280	242	250	318	256
Sodium (d)	g	3.00	2.85	2.95	2.70	3.23	3.17	2.77
Potassium	g	3.05	2.97	3.12	2.73	2.89	3.61	2.91
Thiamin	mg	1.64	1.59	1.66	1.41	1.59	1.87	1.52
Riboflavin	mg	1.88	1.84	1.93	1.69	1.78	2.34	1.85
Niacin equivalent	mg	34.1	32.3	34.6	29.9	32.1	36.9	31.5
Vitamin B6	mg	2.4	2.3	2.4	2.1	2.4	2.7	2.3
Vitamin B12	μg	6.0	6.0	6.3	5.8	6.0	7.8	6.3
Folate	μg	279	270	289	238	256	338	261
Vitamin C	mg	71	68	74	55	67	83	62
Vitamin A:								
Retinol	μg	478	471	508	430	473	740	505
β-carotene	μg	1 894	1 820	1 974	1 607	1 560	2 315	1 701
Retinol equivalent	μg	799	779	841	702	734	1 136	793
Vitamin D	μg	3.11	3.05	3.26	2.95	2.88	4.07	3.01
Vitamin E	mg	11.90	11.78	12.02	12.43	18.85	12.92	12.18
		as a percentage of total food and drink energy excluding alcohol						
Fat	%	37.5	37.3	38.1	39.1	43.3	38.0	38.0
Fatty acids:								
Saturates	%	14.6	14.5	15.0	14.7	15.6	15.4	14.5
Mono-unsaturates	%	13.6	13.5	13.8	14.5	15.8	13.6	13.9
Poly-unsaturates	%	6.7	6.7	6.7	7.4	9.1	6.3	7.0
Carbohydrate	%	48.4	48.9	47.6	47.4	44.4	48.1	48.3
Non-milk extrinsic sugars	%	15.5	15.6	15.1	14.9	13.4	15.7	15.9
Protein	%	14.2	13.9	14.3	13.5	12.3	13.9	13.7

continued

Table 8.14 continued

		Economically active					Economically inactive	
		Full time employees	Part time employees	Self employed	Un-employed	Gov't Training Scheme	Retired	Other
		as a percentage of weighted reference nutrient intake (e)						
Energy (f)	%	95	96	96	91	108	111	95
Energy excluding alcohol (f)	%	91	93	93	88	106	108	93
Protein	%	150	150	154	141	159	158	149
Calcium	%	124	123	126	116	138	145	124
Iron	%	99	96	103	87	93	139	95
Zinc	%	100	100	102	93	109	116	99
Magnesium	%	94	92	95	84	92	102	90
Sodium (d)	%	182	175	179	168	209	179	172
Potassium	%	87	86	89	80	90	93	86
Thiamin	%	174	173	177	151	176	200	167
Riboflavin	%	148	148	152	135	148	179	149
Niacin equivalent	%	218	213	221	193	214	242	209
Vitamin B6	%	177	175	179	158	187	188	171
Vitamin B12	%	391	397	412	387	417	468	423
Folate	%	134	131	139	116	131	153	129
Vitamin C	%	167	161	174	130	164	187	148
Vitamin A (retinol equivalent)	%	116	115	122	103	112	160	117

(a) Contributions from pharmaceutical sources are not recorded by the survey
(b) Available carbohydrate, calculated as monosaccharide equivalent
(c) As non-starch polysaccharides
(d) (i) Excludes sodium from table salt (ii) The RNI for sodium is the amount that is sufficient for 97 per cent of the population. In May 2003 the Scientific Advisory Committee on Nutrition made recommendations about the maximum amount of salt that people should be eating, i.e. that the average salt intake for adults should be no more than 6 grams per day, equivalent to 2.4 grams of sodium per day
(e) Department of Health, 'Dietary Reference Values for Food Energy and Nutrients for the United Kingdom', HMSO 1991
(f) As a percentage of Estimated Average Requirement

The Family Food Committee

We are extremely grateful to the Family Food Committee whose advice on the conduct of the Expenditure and Food Survey and the form of the annual report is invaluable.

Peter HELM (chair)
Department for Environment, Food and Rural Affairs

Bev BOTTING
Office for National Statistics

Professor Judith BUTTRISS
British Nutrition Foundation

Cathy GIBBINS
Office for National Statistics

Professor Andrew CHESHER
University College, London

Dr Kathy JOHNSTON
Scottish Executive Environment and Rural Affairs Department

Francis JONES
Office for National Statistics

Dr Malcolm MEGAW
Department of Agriculture and Rural Development for Northern Ireland

Dr Michael NELSON
Kings College, London

Robert PRICE
Food and Drink Federation

Sheela REDDY
Department of Health

Gillian SWAN
Food Standards Agency

Professor Martin WISEMAN
University of Southampton

Development Issues

The Defra team in conjunction with the Family Food Committee have agreed the following development issues:

(1) assess non-response bias related to diet,

(2) increase response to a minimum of 60 per cent,

(3) improve the 10 per cent estimate for wasted quantities of purchases,

(4) incorporation of free food,

(5) timeliness of results,

(6) updating portion sizes,

(7) updating nutrient profiles,

(8) accuracy of reporting,

(9) lack of standard errors,

(10) accuracy of nutrient profiles.

Progress made in 2005-06

(1) assess non-response bias related to diet
No work was carried out in 2005-06.

(2) increase response to a minimum of 60 per cent
Response on the EFS continues to be a concern with rates in Great Britain being below 60 per cent. For the 2004/05 survey the GB response rate was 57%. This compares with 58% in 2003/04. In Northern Ireland the rate was 52% compared with 58 % in 2003/04. Interview training and briefing on the survey has been regularly reviewed. Recent measures include the introduction of Avoiding Refusal Training (ART). All ONS interviewers completed this training during the summer of 2005. This training is to help interviewers gain co-operation of respondents on the doorstep using advanced communication techniques. The briefings for EFS interviewers have recently been extended to include a day of intensive home study before the face-to-face briefing. During 2005 refresher training took place for experienced EFS interviewers.

(3) improve the 10 per cent estimate for wasted quantities of purchases
Discussions have been held with WRAP (Waste & Resources Action Programme). WRAP is set up as a not-for-profit company limited by guarantee by Defra, the DTI, and the devolved administrations of Scotland, Wales and Northern Ireland. Exploratory research by WRAP in 2005-06 included "quantitative assessment of food waste" and "development of a method for characterising food in the dustbin". In 2006/7 WRAP would like to commission more extensive research that will assess both qualitatively and quantitatively the nature, scale and causes of food waste arising in the UK. This could make use of a wide range of research methods including food waste diaries, householder interviews, waste composition analysis, ethnographic and observation techniques.

(4) incorporation of free food

Defra have made detailed estimates of quantities of free food consumed which are not yet incorporated into the published estimates while quality assurance is carried out. The estimates are based on the numbers of occurrences of free food recorded in the survey. Categories of free food include school fruit, school milk, welfare milk, free school meals, meals provided by employer.

(5) timeliness of results

Timeliness of the UK statistics notice for the survey year 2004-05 was improved by four months with publication in December 2005 compared to April 2005 previously. Timeliness of the annual report Family Food 2004-05 was improved by two months with publication in May 2006 compared to July 2005 previously.

(6) updating portion sizes

No work was carried out in 2005-06.

(7) updating nutrient profiles, incorporating (10) accuracy of nutrient profiles

The Food Standards Agency provides nutrient profiles for the Expenditure and Food Survey. Each food code used in the survey is made up of a number of individual sub-codes to which nutrient and market share data are assigned. The sub-codes that make up a food code represent those foods which contribute a significant proportion of the food code in terms of market share, and have a different nutrient composition to the other sub-codes that comprise a food code. For example, the food code fruit juice comprises a number of sub-codes including grapefruit, orange, pineapple and apple juices. A nutrient profile is calculated for each food code from a weighted average of the sub-codes based on relative market share. Profiles for EFS codes updated for the 2004-05 survey included: spirits with mixer, canned pasta, dried and fresh pasta, sauces, breakfast cereals, oatmeal and oat products, takeaway pasta and noodles, milk, muesli, margarine.

(8) accuracy of reporting

The ONS with help from Defra have addressed the issue of coding errors in the categories of fruit juices and fats and spreads. Defra checks now identify less than 0.5 per cent of codings as errors.

(9) lack of standard errors

Defra have set up an efficient way of calculating simplified standard errors and are now in a position to produce approximate standard errors for quantity and expenditure of all the standard food codes and groups of food codes. The use of reliability indicators has been extended in the annual report. Standard errors for three year averages are being introduced into the datasets.

Plans for 2006-07

For (1) we intend, with the assistance of the ONS, to analyse non-response and non-contact addresses by regional and demographic variables and attempt to shed some light on potential link to diet. At this stage we are not considering a follow up survey of non-respondents.

For (3) we intend to play an active role as a stakeholder in work planned by WRAP on estimating consumer food waste.

For (4) we intend to finish quality assurance work on free food and revise estimates back to 2001-02. A statistics release will be used to announce the revisions.

For (6) we intend to explore options for updating portion sizes to be discussed by the Family Food Committee in 2007.

For (7) we intend to review with the Food Standards Agency our process of converting quantities into energy and nutrient intakes. We intend to publish details of the process including when the nutrient profiles were last updated for each food code.

Links To Family Food Datasets On The Defra Website

United Kingdom

Household purchased quantities:
http://statistics.defra.gov.uk/esg/publications/efs/datasets/efscons.xls

Household expenditure:
http://statistics.defra.gov.uk/esg/publications/efs/datasets/efsexpd.xls

Household energy and nutrient intakes:
http://statistics.defra.gov.uk/esg/publications/efs/datasets/efsnutr.xls

Household energy and nutrient intakes by food type:
http://statistics.defra.gov.uk/esg/publications/efs/datasets/efsnutsfood.xls

Eating out purchased quantities and expenditure:
http://statistics.defra.gov.uk/esg/publications/efs/datasets/eoconsexpd.xls

Eating out energy and nutrient intakes:
http://statistics.defra.gov.uk/esg/publications/efs/datasets/eonutrients.xls

Eating out energy and nutrient intakes by food type:
http://statistics.defra.gov.uk/esg/publications/efs/datasets/eonutsfoods.xls

UK regions

Household purchased quantities:
http://statistics.defra.gov.uk/esg/publications/efs/datasets/gorcons.xls

Household expenditure:
http://statistics.defra.gov.uk/esg/publications/efs/datasets/gorexp.xls

Household energy and nutrient intakes:
http://statistics.defra.gov.uk/esg/publications/efs/datasets/gornutr.xls

Eating out purchased quantities and expenditure:
http://statistics.defra.gov.uk/esg/publications/efs/datasets/eogorconexp.xls

Eating out energy and nutrient intakes:
http://statistics.defra.gov.uk/esg/publications/efs/datasets/eogornutr.xls

Income quintiles

Household purchased quantities:
http://statistics.defra.gov.uk/esg/publications/efs/datasets/quintcons.xls

Household expenditure:
http://statistics.defra.gov.uk/esg/publications/efs/datasets/quintexp.xls

Household energy and nutrient intakes:
http://statistics.defra.gov.uk/esg/publications/efs/datasets/quintnutr.xls

Eating out purchased quantities and expenditure:
http://statistics.defra.gov.uk/esg/publications/efs/datasets/eoquintconexp.xls

Eating out energy and nutrient intakes:
http://statistics.defra.gov.uk/esg/publications/efs/datasets/eoquintnutr.xls

Household composition

Household purchased quantities:
http://statistics.defra.gov.uk/esg/publications/efs/datasets/hhcompcons.xls

Household expenditure:
http://statistics.defra.gov.uk/esg/publications/efs/datasets/hhcompexp.xls

Household energy and nutrient intakes:
http://statistics.defra.gov.uk/esg/publications/efs/datasets/hhcompnutr.xls

Eating out purchased quantities and expenditure:
http://statistics.defra.gov.uk/esg/publications/efs/datasets/eohhcompconexp.xls

Eating out energy and nutrient intakes:
http://statistics.defra.gov.uk/esg/publications/efs/datasets/eohhcompnutr.xls

Income quintile and household composition

Household purchased quantities:
http://statistics.defra.gov.uk/esg/publications/efs/datasets/hhcompxinccons.xls

Household expenditure:
http://statistics.defra.gov.uk/esg/publications/efs/datasets/hhcompxincexp.xls

Household energy and nutrient intakes:
http://statistics.defra.gov.uk/esg/publications/efs/datasets/hhcompxincnutr.xls

Eating out purchased quantities and expenditure:
http://statistics.defra.gov.uk/esg/publications/efs/datasets/eohhcompxincconexpd.xls

Eating out energy and nutrient intakes:
http://statistics.defra.gov.uk/esg/publications/efs/datasets/eohhcompxincnutr.xls

Age group of household reference person

Household purchased quantities:
http://statistics.defra.gov.uk/esg/publications/efs/datasets/agehrpcons.xls

Household expenditure:
http://statistics.defra.gov.uk/esg/publications/efs/datasets/agehrpexp.xls

Household energy and nutrient intakes:
http://statistics.defra.gov.uk/esg/publications/efs/datasets/agehrpnutr.xls

Eating out purchased quantities and expenditure:
http://statistics.defra.gov.uk/esg/publications/efs/datasets/eoagehrpconexp.xls

Eating out energy and nutrient intakes:
http://statistics.defra.gov.uk/esg/publications/efs/datasets/eoagehrpnutr.xls

Age at which household reference person ceased full-time education

Household purchased quantities:
http://statistics.defra.gov.uk/esg/publications/efs/datasets/agehrpedcons.xls

Household expenditure:
http://statistics.defra.gov.uk/esg/publications/efs/datasets/agehrpedexp.xls

Household energy and nutrient intakes:
http://statistics.defra.gov.uk/esg/publications/efs/datasets/agehrpednutr.xls

Eating out purchased quantities and expenditure:
http://statistics.defra.gov.uk/esg/publications/efs/datasets/eoagehrpedconexp.xls

Eating out energy and nutrient intakes:
http://statistics.defra.gov.uk/esg/publications/efs/datasets/eoagehrpednutr.xls

Ethnic origin of household reference person

Household purchased quantities and expenditure:
http://statistics.defra.gov.uk/esg/publications/efs/datasets/ethohrpconsexp.xls

Household energy and nutrient intakes:
http://statistics.defra.gov.uk/esg/publications/efs/datasets/ethohrpnutr.xls

Eating out purchased quantities and expenditure:
http://statistics.defra.gov.uk/esg/publications/efs/datasets/eoethohrpconexp.xls

Eating out energy and nutrient intakes:
http://statistics.defra.gov.uk/esg/publications/efs/datasets/eoethohrpnutr.xls

Socio-economic classification of household reference person

Household purchased quantities and expenditure:
http://statistics.defra.gov.uk/esg/publications/efs/datasets/nssecconsexp.xls

Household energy and nutrient intakes:
http://statistics.defra.gov.uk/esg/publications/efs/datasets/nssecnutr.xls

Eating out purchased quantities and expenditure:
http://statistics.defra.gov.uk/esg/publications/efs/datasets/eonssechrpconexp.xls

Eating out energy and nutrient intakes:
http://statistics.defra.gov.uk/esg/publications/efs/datasets/eonssechrpnutr.xls

Economic activity of household reference person

Household purchased quantities and expenditure:
http://statistics.defra.gov.uk/esg/publications/efs/datasets/econactconsexp.xls

Household energy and nutrient intakes:
http://statistics.defra.gov.uk/esg/publications/efs/datasets/econactnutr.xls

Eating out purchased quantities and expenditure:
http://statistics.defra.gov.uk/esg/publications/efs/datasets/eoeconactconexp.xls

Eating out energy and nutrient intakes:
http://statistics.defra.gov.uk/esg/publications/efs/datasets/eoeconactnutr.xls